IT ALL STARTED
WITH EUROPA

It all started with EUROPA

BEING AN UNDIGESTED HISTORY OF EUROPE
FROM PREHISTORIC MAN TO THE PRESENT,
PROVING THAT WE REMEMBER BEST
WHATEVER IS LEAST IMPORTANT

BY RICHARD ARMOUR

WITH APPROPRIATELY ABSURD ILLUSTRATIONS
BY *Campbell Grant*

MC GRAW-HILL BOOK COMPANY, INC.

NEW YORK   TORONTO   LONDON

FIRST PRINTING AUGUST, 1955
SECOND PRINTING SEPTEMBER, 1955
THIRD PRINTING DECEMBER, 1955
FOURTH PRINTING AUGUST, 1956
FIFTH PRINTING DECEMBER, 1957
SIXTH PRINTING JULY, 1959
SEVENTH PRINTING MARCH, 1962
EIGHTH PRINTING JULY, 1963
NINTH PRINTING MARCH, 1966
TENTH PRINTING MARCH, 1967
ELEVENTH PRINTING DECEMBER, 1968

02247

Library of Congress Catalog Card Number: 55–9532

Published by the McGraw-Hill Book Company, Inc.
Printed in the United States of America

DEDICATED

to history students and history teachers,
who for generations have made
each other equally unhappy

ACKNOWLEDGMENTS

The author is pleased to acknowledge that he has made no use whatever of the works of Thucydides, Tacitus, Gibbon, and Arnold J. Toynbee. He is also grateful to his wife, who has unflaggingly refused assistance. Above all, he wishes to thank his forebears, to whom he is indebted for the strain of insanity without which this book would not have been so impossible.

R.A.

CAUTIONARY NOTE
ANY RESEMBLANCE BETWEEN THIS
BOOK AND THE WORK OF ANY OTHER
HISTORIAN, LIVING OR DEAD, IS
HIGHLY UNLIKELY.

CHAPTER I

EUROPE AT THE BEGINNING

THE BEGINNINGS of Europe are shrouded in impenetrable myths. According to one of these, Europe was named after Europa, a girl who rode around on a bull named Jupiter. The fact that Jupiter was actually not a bull but a god (see the Greeks and Romans, below) gives us some indication of the uncertainty of those early days. All Europa knew was that it was transportation.

Except for lending her name, Europa had little to do with Western civilization. Some scholars, however, detect her influence on Far Western culture, notably the custom of riding the bull at rodeos and slinging it at dude ranches and Bar-B-Qs.[1]

Europe is also called the Old Country, the Old World, and Where My People Came From. People who live in Europe are called Europeans until they emigrate to America, where they are called Foreigners.

GEOGRAPHY AND CLIMATE

Europe, like the rest of the Earth, was originally too hot to handle. It had no sooner cooled off than it was covered by ice as far as the eye could see, and even farther. The northernmost region was populated by Ice Men who carried ice picks and traveled in ice packs. It was generally agreed that what Europe needed was a good thaw, but while everybody talked about it, nobody did anything. Waiting for the ice to retreat to the north,

---

[1] For "slinging the bull," see *American Dictionary of Colorful and Off-Colorful Expressions.*

a few inches a year, the Europeans grew increasingly impatient. They were eager to discover places like Norway and Sweden and to see their first Great Dane.

After the ice left, Europe was covered with dense forests, which first had to be cleared and later carefully preserved. The forests could hardly be seen because of the trees, and were full of fierce animals ready to spring, and fierce birds ready to chirp. Lakes, dug out by glaciers, provided our European ancestors with picturesque scenery and healthful spas. To these latter they went to take the baths, which they badly needed, and to recover from the gout, an ailment which it was as much fun to get as to get over.

In those days, which were extremely B.C.,[1] England was part of Europe, and Ireland, much to the disgust of the Irish, was part of England. Owing to the absence of the English Channel, channel swimming was virtually unknown.

The disgust of the Irish

Europe and Africa were still connected at Gibraltar, which was of no strategic importance and therefore not held by the British. Maps were very poor, and it was hard to distinguish Asia Minor from Asia Major and Asia Proper from Asia Im-

[1] Before Continents.

proper. The largest region was the Unknown World, an area not yet Ripe for Conquest and Colonialization.

———◆———

CHAPTER II

PREHISTORIC MAN

ACCORDING TO DARWIN, the first men hung from the branches of trees by their tails. It was not until much later that they discovered ropes and began to hang each other. For some reason, our ancestors' tails got shorter and shorter, and the fun gradually went out of swinging. Whether or not men descended from monkeys, as soon as they lost their tails they descended from trees.

The earliest Europeans were Homo Sapiens, Neanderthal, and Cro-Magnon. The latter, because of his hyphenated name, was probably British. Little is known of these original men,[1] except that Homo Sapiens was the brightest and Cro-Magnon had a long head. Nothing favorable has ever been said about Neanderthal, although his masculinity was unquestioned. He had the hairiest chest until Ernest Hemingway.

Hairiest chest until Hemingway

---

[1] Those who were even more original are referred to as aboriginal.

3

After the Ice Age came the Stone Age. Stones had certain advantages over ice. For instance:

1. They were warmer, especially when left in the sun.
2. They didn't melt on the way home.
3. They gave employment to stone masons and made possible the naming of Stonewall Jackson.

On the other hand, they were inferior to ice in certain respects:

1. They were no good for highballs.[1]
2. They were unsatisfactory for skating on.

Fortunately, stones were plentiful. Furthermore, there was little or no depreciation, and a used stone was as good as a brand-new one. Geology was in its infancy, and rock gardening was unknown.

LIFE IN THESE EARLY TIMES

We must not suppose that Europeans of the Stone Age felt thwarted by their failure to discover bronze and iron. Whittling away thoughtfully on stones, hunting wild beasts and women, they kept busy. The more energetic of them left no stone unturned.

Let us picture the daily life of one of our ancestors. Rising early, perhaps awakened by the dripping of water from a stalactite directly overhead, he makes his toilet by untangling his hair from his eyebrows and rubbing a small stone over his well-developed incisors, being careful to use an up-and-down stroke. He has a light breakfast of roots, berries, and raw mastodon meat,[2] completely unaware that every mouthful is bursting with vitamins.

Pulling the rumpled earth back into place, he makes his bed. This is woman's work, he thinks, and is reminded of his day's chores. He must find a double-breasted animal to skin for a new suit, and a woman, similarly endowed, to be his mate.

[1] Unless, as some contend, the phrase "on the rocks" was coined by a Stone Age bartender.

[2] The Large Economy Size.

4

With a quick backward glance at his cave, and making a mental note to arch the top of his doorway a little, like his neighbor's, he is off on his appointed rounds. Avoiding the brontosauruses and thesauruses, which are a bit large for his purpose, he searches out a saber-toothed tiger and removes the skin.[1] Unless he has in mind military regalia, he also removes the saber.

The woman is a little more of a problem, but not much. Our ancestor has a poor posture, his forehead is repellent to those who prefer the intellectual type, and his teeth cry out for the attention of an orthodontist. But there is something exciting about the way he can beat a woman over the head with a club. He knows the right spot, just above the ears, and his blows have a certain manly authority about them. By mid-afternoon he has clubbed a smart-looking brunette into a swoon. Taking her silence to mean assent, he seizes her by the forelock, or anything handy, and drags her away. Whatever skin comes off along the road, he says to himself, will grow back.

Long lapels

As the shadows of late afternoon lengthen, our ancestor and his bride arrive home, unencumbered by rice or old shoes. He carries her over the threshold of the cave and tenderly drops

[1] First killing the tiger, if necessary.

5

her. The honeymoon is over. As soon as she regains consciousness, she assumes her wifely duties, cutting the tiger skin into long lapels and natural shoulders, preparing a supper of leftover mastodon meat, and enlarging the dug-out portion of the floor to make a double bed.

Little does our ancestor think, as he nestles his head into the clod that serves as his pillow, that in a few thousand years men will be urged to return to nature. He, although he does not appreciate his good fortune, is already there.

ARTS AND CRAFTS

Paintings were usually done right on the walls of caves, to save the expense of framing. Nude portraits were popular, especially those of deer and bison. But, since this was the dawn of civilization, the light was poor, and artists were unable to do their best work. They were scornfully called Primitives by those who knew nothing about art but knew what they liked. In terms of years, if not ability, Primitives must be considered the genuine Old Masters.

Primitive art

As the shapes and sizes of stones improved, craftsmen made spectacular advances in such fields as wood carving, meat carving, and murder.

We owe much to prehistoric man. It does not seem likely, however, that we can ever repay him.

———◆———

CHAPTER III

EGYPT AND ITS ENVIRONS

IMPROBABLE AS IT may sound, the cradle of European civilization was the Mediterranean basin. Since this was used by the Sumerians, Egyptians, Babylonians, Assyrians, Medes, and Persians, conditions soon became crowded and unhygienic. It is no wonder that some people became nomadic and were asked to leave. Those who stayed behind sank into a rut and ultimately became fossils.

The Mediterranean Basin

EGYPTIAN ECONOMY

The most important country of this region was Egypt, which owed its prosperity to sand. Large quantities of this valuable

7

substance were shipped all over Europe for use in hourglasses.[1]

Egypt's prosperity came to an end, however, with the invention of the watch, which kept time better without sand. From the lowliest sand-sifter to the head of the Sinister Sand Syndicate, everyone was hard hit. Until the advent of sandpaper, there was almost no demand for Egypt's principal product. The Great Depression, known locally as the Seven Lean Years, set in.

Although we shall make no attempt to trace the ups and dunes of Egypt's economy, we must remark that sand continued to play a significant role. Large areas of it were rented out for use in making motion pictures about the Foreign Legion. Some diversification was achieved by building pyramids. These ancient structures provide interesting backgrounds for middle-aged tourists, whom they make look younger.

Another tourist attraction is a statue called the Sphinx, a bust. The most busted part is the nose. The Sphinx has been standing for thousands of years, but what it stands for is still unknown. It may represent the aspiration of Man to keep his head out of the sand and his mouth shut.

THE NILE VALLEY

The greatest river of Egypt was the Nile, which started at the Alpha and ran as far as the Delta. It would have gone farther but for the Mediterranean.

Each year this river overflowed its banks and fertilized the fields of the Nile Valley with tons of rich dark soil and rich dark Egyptians. Digging side by side with the Egyptian farmers were British archeologists, who could be distinguished by their monocles and pith helmets. If an archeologist occasionally dropped dead, it was because he had contracted the dread disease of the region, Egyptology.

THE PHARAOHS

Egypt was ruled for centuries by Pharaohs. As their statues reveal, these ruthless kings [2] were exceedingly vain about their

---

[1] *I.e.*, the sands of time.

[2] Their only rival for cruelty was Nebuchadnezzar, in neighboring Babylonia, who was always hanging gardeners.

profiles. When not posing for sculptors, the Pharaohs were busy worshiping the sun. The only time off they had was on cloudy days.

For recreation, the Pharaohs enjoyed hiding articles where archeologists would have trouble finding them, and practicing sneers and haughty looks in front of full-length mirrors. Occasionally they would stroll around to see what progress was being made on their tombs.

Pharaoh practicing a haughty look

The Pharaohs had an obsession for building pyramids. These were stone structures that were large at the bottom and got smaller and smaller at the top,[1] because their builders got tired. During their construction, workers had to carry up huge stones weighing as much as five thousand pounds or risk the Pharaoh's displeasure. Most considered a rupture the lesser of two evils.

The pyramids served no useful purpose except for burying Pharaohs. To Egyptians who had been held down for years by a Pharaoh, there was some satisfaction in knowing that the Pharaoh was at last held down by a pyramid.[2]

[1] This was also true of many of the Pharaohs.
[2] See James Hilton's touching farewell, *Goodbye, Mr. Cheops.*

Cleopatra, the great Queen of Egypt, was in many ways unlike the Pharaohs. For one thing, she was prettier. For another, she specialized in couches instead of pyramids. She spent most of her life reclining on one side, and after thirty years was the victim of what her physician called Side-Saddle Sores. What with the flies and the heat, Cleopatra loved to be fanned, and her servants started the first Fan Club. About the only thing she exercised, during all her years as the recumbent, were her eyelashes and her authority.

Cleopatra was the quiet type, yet thought of herself as a siren. She possessed a certain attraction for men, and soon had them eating out of her hand, although some admitted privately that they preferred plates. Men also had a certain attraction for Cleopatra, especially those with armies larger than her own.

Even the great Julius Caesar came under her spell.[1] It seemed like a good match: she had youth and beauty, and Caesar had the Roman Empire. Cleopatra went to Rome, but Caesar's death and a close look at Mark Antony changed her plans. She took a slow barge to Egypt, and Antony followed on her heels.[2]

Caesar and Cleopatra

[1] Cleopatra tried to teach him hieroglyphics, but he was too old to learn.
[2] A part of her anatomy overlooked by historians and artists.

Antony and Cleopatra might have been happy together, but in Egypt's torrid climate fate perspired against them. They both committed suicide, Antony requesting permission to die in Cleopatra's arms, where he felt right at home. Cleopatra, ingenious even in death, was bitten in the end by an asp.[1]

On his death bed (*i.e.*, his and Cleopatra's), Antony deliriously called her "Egypt." He probably confused her with the gently rolling countryside.

If there is a moral to the story of Cleopatra, it is that a queen can get only so far in a reclining position.

THE CONTRIBUTIONS OF EGYPT

Egypt bequeathed rich gifts to European civilization. These included:

1. Papyrus, a material which was almost as good as paper, but too heavy for air mail.
2. Mummies, people who were all wrapped up in themselves.
3. Ra, an indispensable part of college cheers.

———◆———

CHAPTER IV

ANCIENT GREECE

THE ANCIENT GREEKS were industrious people. They produced so many urns, vases, and philosophers that Europe was overstocked for centuries. Thanks to their enormous vocabulary, they had a word for everything. Indeed, civilization reached such a high point in ancient Greece that it had no place to go but down.

GREEK WARS

The Greeks were a peace-loving people who were almost constantly at war. This was a lucky thing for historians such as Herodotus, Thucydides, and Xylophone, who wrote vivid eyewitness accounts of battles as soon as they had read up on them.

[1] Whatever happened to the asp is one of the mysteries of history.

One of the great battles was at Marathon, where the Greeks outran the Persians. The Greeks had been secretly training for this battle in their Olympic games, in which runners in hot pursuit of one another carried torches. As the Persians discovered, it was no fun to be ahead, because you got scorched behind.

The Battle of Marathon

In another campaign, the Greeks were less successful. They pitted their columns (Doric, Ionic, and Corinthian) against the phalanxes and philippics of Philip of Macedon. The Greek columns were badly pitted when Philip got through with them, as anyone may see today.

What Philip failed to do to the Greeks was done by his son, Alexander the Great, who spread Greek culture all over the world and thereby dangerously thinned it out at home. Alexander was the first emperor with sufficient nerve to declare himself a god, although many of his predecessors had felt much the same way about themselves.

The Greeks had an army and a navy, but no air force except a couple of queer birds named Icarus and Daedalus, who flew around on borrowed wings fastened with wax. Icarus ran out of wax and fell into the sea.

THE SPARTANS

Most of the wars in Greece were caused by the Spartans, who were ill at ease when they were not fighting. The Spartans specialized in pain; they considered it heroic to be stoic.

Spartan life began early. If a Spartan baby was unathletic and had narrow shoulders, he was taken into the mountains and exposed to the elements. If he crawled back home, he was taken out and exposed again. Double exposure was usually sufficient.

A Spartan leader reclined at night on a bed of boards,[1] from which he arose in the morning refreshed and full of splinters.

A Spartan arising

Two hours of calisthenics and a cold shower worked up an enormous appetite for breakfast, which he skipped. The day was given over to toughening exercises, such as sitting on spears and munching nails. Immediately after an uneaten lunch there were breath-holding contests. The man who held his breath longest was promised the top spot on the funeral pyre.

In the evening the Spartan families gathered convivially around the fire and occasionally stuck in a hand or a foot for a couple of minutes. From time to time they felt each other's muscles. Children listened attentively to father's account of how he won the village finger-flexing championship when *he* was a boy.

So the days passed, full of wholesome fun and whole-wheat bread. It was a hard life, and that was the way they liked it. The Spartans allowed themselves only one luxury. That was being carried around on their shields when they were dead.

[1] See the expression "room and board."

13

Greek art reached its peak under Pericles. All the artists were classical, and every work of art was a classic. It was called the Golden Age, for prestige purposes, although everything was actually made of marble.

Sculptors included such famous names as Phidias and Perphidias. Nor should we forget Praxiteles and Prophylaxis. It was Phidias who was responsible for the impediment on the Parthenon, which Lord Elgin wisely took to England, where they needed beautiful things to make up for their women. This same Englishman owned the Elgin Marbles, with which Keats played as a boy.

Most of the Greek statues depicted Venus, a goddess who spent most of her time posing. Her proportions, which have always appealed to lovers of the finer things, were on the generous side. Or perhaps the Greek sculptors got tired of hacking away all day at marble. In some statues of Venus the arms are missing. Armless, with her dress sliding down, she has a helpless look that goes straight to the heart of the male observer.

That helpless look

The men in Greek statues are usually throwing discuses, picking thorns out of their feet, struggling with snakes, or dying of gaul trouble. They are invariably clad in the simple, severely classical fig leaf, considered correct for daytime wear but a little cool in the evening. The art of wearing a fig leaf without suspenders was lost with the Greeks.

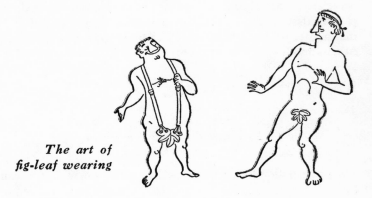

The art of fig-leaf wearing

GREEK LITERATURE

The greatest writer in Ancient Greece was Homer, the author of the *Iliadnoddyssey*. It was Homer who discovered that the best place to begin an epic is in the middle, so that you are never far from either end.

Two characters who continue to come alive for the modern reader, although they have been dead for several thousand years, are Helen of Troy and Achilles. Helen is best known for having launched a thousand ships with her face. Despite the wear and tear, she was still beautiful enough to be missed by her husband when she was carried off by Paris, a handsome young Trojan of French extraction who thought married women were more interesting. This led to all sorts of ill-fated consequences, none of them more serious than Homer's epic about the event.

As for Achilles, he was a famous warrior who rose to great heights by wearing elevator shoes which gave him a sore heel. He nursed his wrath and his heel in a tent during most of the battle, with only an occasional peep through the tent flaps to see how nearly it was over. Meanwhile Homer, in a nearby tent, sang of Achilles' exploits and kept everyone awake.[1]

Before we leave Greek literature, we should not fail to mention the advances made by the three classic unities, Aeschylus, Sophocles, and Euripides, whose writings were exceedingly gloomy despite the presence of a chorus. It was of Euripides that a later poet penned the famous lines about a gentleman of Athens and his visit to a tailor:

> *Knock, knock.*
> *Who's there?*
> *Euripides.*
> *Euripides who?*
> *Euripides pants and I won't*
>   *bring you another pair.*

An alternate version, perhaps having to do with a second pair of pants, contains the matchless dialogue: "Eumenides pants?" "Yes, Euripides?" All of these tragic writers wrote tragedies in which the hero died because of (1) tragic fate, (2) a flaw in his character, or (3) a nasty stab. According to Aristotle, watching such a play was a moving experience and had a cathartic effect. Students agree that the best plays of these writers have been lost.

THE GREEK PHILOSOPHERS

Everyone thought a great deal, but those who thought professionally were called Philosophers, or Muses. Most of them taught in one of the Schools of Thought. Occasionally, after too much thinking, a Muse would blow a fuse.

It is generally assumed that Aristotle was an Aristotelian and Plato was a Platonist. Plato's greatest contribution was known as Platonic Love, or Strictly Platonic, which through the centuries has proved a helpful device for bachelors seeking to avoid entanglements.

[1] Among the Memorable Phrases coined by Homer is "Never look a Trojan horse in the mouth."

16

Almost everyone in Athens knew Socrates, especially Socrates, whose motto was "Know thyself." He once described himself as "a gad-fly on the rump of the state," a position to which he clung tenaciously, even when sat on.

Socrates was forever talking. In fact he talked so much he never had time to write anything down, and Plato had to follow him around with a pad and pencil. He liked to ask people questions of which he alone knew the answers. While he didn't learn much this way, he could always dominate the conversation. The only person who outtalked Socrates was Xantippe, his wife. Xantippe was a shrew. She had a sharp tongue, which she carried around instead of a pocketknife and used for making cutting remarks. It is said that Socrates stayed with Xantippe in order to develop his self-control. No one has been able to explain why Xantippe stayed with Socrates.

Eventually Socrates' talking got him into trouble. He was accused of having corrupted the youth of Athens by making them waste time thinking. He finally stopped talking long enough to drink a glass of hemlock juice. Unlike his patient listeners, this disagreed with him.[1]

OTHER GREAT GREEKS

Not all the Greeks were sculptors and philosophers. One of those who had another occupation was Euclid, who is generally blamed for geometry. Another was Hippocrates, the originator of the Hippocritical Oath, still adhered to by physicians who tell a patient that it won't hurt. Yet another was Damocles, who walked around with a sword suspended over his head. (The suspense was terrible.) There was also Archimedes, a prying sort of fellow, who invented the crowbar. He also discovered Specific Gravity, which he defined as "the opposite of General Hilarity." Finally there was Diogenes, who spent his nights walking the streets with a lantern, looking for an honest man, apparently not realizing that all such people were home in bed.

[1] Socrates' last words are said to have been the much-quoted exclamation, "Gosh all hemlock!"

Damocles

THE LEGACY OF GREECE

We are indebted to the Greeks for Greek theaters, Greek fraternities, Greek restaurants, and such Memorable Expressions as "It's all Greek to me."

———◆———

CHAPTER V

THE RISE OF ROME

ROME WAS FOUNDED by two boys, Romulus and Remus, who were as hard to tell apart as Gilbert and Sullivan. When they were very small, they were left outdoors to fend for themselves, and were a couple of badly battered fenders by the time they were found by a passing wolf. The wolf took them home to his wife, who had an extra pair of nipples to which Romulus and Remus in time became attached. After many years of drinking wolf's milk, they grew up to be big, hairy fellows and full of calcium.

As time went on, they began hearing the Call of Destiny.

A tearful leave

Taking a tearful leave of the wolf and a last long drink (one for the road), they set out. Since all roads led to Rome, they founded the city without difficulty.

THE WOMAN PROBLEM

Women were scarce in early Rome. There were of course the Vestal Virgins, but they were a cold lot even though they were always tending fires.

So the men of Rome were forced to import the Sabine women. These ladies were heavy-set, especially where they sat, and exactly to the taste of Romulus, Remus, and Rubens. Women were no longer a problem, or at least not in the same way.

No doubt it was a woman who caused Remus, by now middle-aged and known as Uncle Remus, to leave Rome and go to live with Peter Rabbit in a briar patch.

THE GODS

To keep on the good side of the gods, the Romans sacrificed lambs, cows, and such people as they felt they could spare. The gods were thought to be connected with fertility, especially by means of a lightly clad goddess named Ceres, who signified plenty.

Foremost among the gods was Jupiter. He was married to Juno, but had most of his children with the help of other women. An exception was Minerva. After a severe attack of

19

migraine, she sprang from his forehead fully grown and wearing a suit of armor. Even among the gods, this sort of thing was unusual. Jupiter ultimately retired to Mount Olympus and spent his declining years puttering around with thunderbolts.

Venus was the goddess of love, but had no monopoly.

Justice was a blind goddess who had scales. Critics thought there was something fishy about this.

Mercury had wings growing out of his feet and thus could wear nothing but open-side sandals.

We should not fail to mention Neptune, who inhabited the ocean. Swimmers had to be on guard, since he had a habit of suddenly coming up for air with his pitchfork held on high.

And finally there was Bacchus, the god of wine, who was always laughing and leering. He usually carried around a bunch of grapes, thinking he might happen on a wine press. Bacchus was accompanied by a crowd of young men and women who acted as if they were walking home from a late party, having been told they had better not drive. Some of the men were part goat, but the others were too far gone to notice.

Everything was in the lap of the gods, and there was no telling what would happen when they stood up.

GOVERNMENT OF ROME

Rome was ruled by a Triumvirate. This consisted of three men who spent most of their time plotting to kill each other.

Triumvirate

They refused to believe that three heads were better than one. Some of these leaders became elder statesmen, many of them centurions and even older.

There was a Senate, but no House, and there were pro-consuls but no anti-consuls. A farmer had as good a chance to be elected to high office as a lawyer does today. An instance of this was Cincinnatus, an Ohioan who was drafted for office while plowing. After serving a term, he went back to his plow and finished the furrow. This was the beginning of crop rotation: one year a farmer, one year a politician.

ROMAN WARS

Until Julius Caesar, fighting was on a small scale. There were, for instance, the Puny Wars, fought against Carthage. The high point of these conflicts came when Hannibal crossed the Alps with an army of elephants. He would have taken Rome, but ran out of peanuts. Hannibal is remembered long after most generals, probably because elephants have such good memories. The nearest thing to elephants, previously, had been battering rams, used to knock on the gates of cities until somebody came.

Rome produced many brave warriors. One of these was Horatius, who stood on a bridge taking a toll of the enemy. While he stood there, the crafty Romans demolished the bridge, and Horatius, in full armor, did a half gainer with a quarter twist into the river below. To compensate him for rust and loss of face, the Romans first dried him off and then pensioned him off.

LIFE IN ANCIENT ROME

The Romans were extremely systematic. They divided people into two kinds, patricians and plebeians. Then they divided all the hard work into two equal parts, both of which they allotted to the plebeians.

The patricians wore a simple, loose-fitting garment that wrapped around rather nonchalantly and was called the toga, or the sack of Rome.

21

Much of the home life of Rome centered in the home, where the father was surrounded by an admiring family and innumerable busts (of himself). The head of the house, usually named Pater, ate lying on a couch, since food made him sleepy and he wanted to be ready.

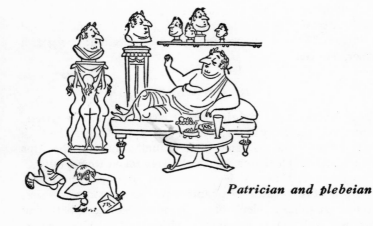

Patrician and plebeian

The Romans had a passion for cleanliness. They gathered in large public baths and soaked until time to eat, after which they waited barely the required hour to avoid cramps before getting back in. Saturday was a Roman holiday, and the baths were so crowded that it was impossible to stretch out full length. Most Romans tested the temperature of the water with their servants' toes first. It was no good to ask somebody who was already in. He might be a Stoic.

In addition to baths, the Romans had a great fondness for chariot races and games. The Big Game was usually held in the Colosseum. Between halves, entertainment was provided by lions and Christians, who put on an act together. In the case of the Christians it was a disappearing act. The crowds roared, as did the lions.

When Romans attending the show jerked their thumbs upward, it didn't mean they wanted a ride in a chariot.

22

Disappearing act

JULIUS CAESAR

The greatest of the Roman emperors was Julius Caesar, who led his legions all over Europe. Everywhere he went, he built roads and triumphal arches so that he could get back to Rome quickly and triumphantly if he had to. He especially enjoyed conquering Gaul, which he divided into three parts: Veni, Vidi, and Vici.

Julius Caesar was not only a conqueror but a reformer and a writer. He reformed the calendar, which had been acting up, and was the first general to write his memoirs, thus setting a precedent that too many have followed. This work, which he wrote in Latin, has not yet been completely translated, but school children all over the world are still struggling with it.[1]

Caesar also drained marshes, by pulling out the plug, invented the Caesarean, a new way to give birth, and made laws forbidding nearly everything.

In his later years, Caesar became a bit stout and unwell. A soothsayer came to him and said the sooth: it would be unhealthy for him to go out on the Ides of March.[2] Nevertheless

[1] Other writers include Virgil and Horace, whose last names have been forgotten; Taciturn, an extremely quiet man; and Juvenal, the author of several books for children.

[2] March 15—*Incomum Taxum Deum*. March was a tricky month anyhow. It sometimes came in like a lion and went out like a Christian.

Caesar went out, and before night was lying dead in a rented toga. One of the rents was made by his good friend Brutus, toward whom Caesar had always been particularly generous. On one memorable occasion, when offering his friend a plate of figs or something, he characteristically said, "Eat two, Brutus."

But Brutus, though blinded by tears, managed to find an unused place on Caesar's chest. He knew Mark Antony had prepared a brilliant funeral oration, and was anxious to lend an ear.

CHAPTER VI

THE DECLINE AND FALL OF ROME

AFTER CAESAR came Mark Antony. He went to his downfall with Cleopatra (see above), which must have been better than going there alone. After Mark Antony came Augustus and after Augustus came Tiberius. Somebody was always coming after somebody else, and usually getting him.

The rise of Rome had been gradual and slow. Expressed graphically, it would look something like this:

The decline of Rome was also gradual and only a little faster. It may be diagrammed as follows:

The fall of Rome, however, was more like this:

The last days of Rome were not as dramatic as the last days of Pompeii, mainly because Rome was farther from Mount Vesuvius. According to Gibbon, the English historian, the

24

Romans declined a little bit every day until they were lying helplessly on the floor. The one thing they couldn't decline was food. It was also their practice of Premeditated Regurgitation that weakened their Moral Fiber, to say nothing of their stomachs.

THE BARBARIANS

North of Rome, meanwhile, Europe was full of barbarians, waiting for the Romans to soften up.

The leading barbarians were:

1. *The Goths.* These restless warriors traveled light, but managed to carry destruction wherever they went. They also carried stones, mortar, and flying buttresses with which to build the Gothic cathedrals which still dot the landscape. Under the leadership of Alaric, they sacked Rome in 410, which was considered good time.

2. *The Sloths.* Some of these were three-toed and others were all thumbs. They were lazier than the Goths and less destructive than the Moths.

3. *The Huns.* It has been said that the Huns were not far removed from animals, probably referring to the fact that they were always on horseback. The most famous leader of the Huns was Attila, an ugly little man with bowlegs and a long mustache. Although he carried a spear and a club, he had only to turn his face toward the enemy and there was a mass flight. Against an especially stubborn foe he might have to show his teeth. He was known as the "Scourge of God," but actually caused men more trouble. For a time Attila kept well to the north, for fear of contracting Roman civilization, but finally he decided to risk it. It was lucky for the Romans, and certainly for his bride, that he died on his wedding night.

If the reader is saddened to learn that the uncouth, unkempt barbarians finally overcame the couth, kempt Romans, it may be helpful to remember that the Romans themselves were barbarians once. What was needed was fresh blood, and the barbarians were the ones to supply it.[1]

[1] We have made no mention of the Vandals, which is perhaps just as well.

*The uncouth
and the couth*

OUR DEBT TO THE BARBARIANS

The barbarians hastened the decline and fall of the Roman Empire, much to the relief of Gibbon. They also made significant improvements in the techniques of sacking, pillaging, and plundering. Most important, perhaps, was their development of the Dark Ages, without which it would be difficult to keep Ancient History and Medieval History apart.

FIRST TEST

1. What subject was taught in place of history in prehistoric times?

2. Can you mention the Medes without mentioning the Persians?

3. Estimate the amount of hay that would be required to lose Cleopatra's Needle in a haystack.

4. Is it true that the builders of the pyramids were slow about coming to the point?

5. When the Egyptians gritted their teeth, was it an indication of (*a*) determination or (*b*) a sandstorm?

6. Since most of the Greeks were simple people, what made Oedipus complex?

7. Which of the following do you think caused Socrates more trouble:

    (*a*) Hemlock?

    (*b*) Wedlock?

8. If the Romans took so many years to decline, how long do you think it took them to conjugate?

9. Considering how much walking the Romans did, what explains the fact that so few of their arches have fallen?

CHAPTER VII

THE FRANKS, OF WHOM CHARLEMAGNE WAS THE FRANKEST

THE FIRST Franks [1] were shadowy figures with long mustaches and short tempers. These ancestors of the French had an un-mistakably German look, and it would not be surprising if they were originally Frankfurters. The Frankish men would have been indignant if anyone had hinted that in a few centuries they would be wearing powdered wigs and carrying lace handkerchiefs. The Frankish women looked very little like Madame de Pompadour and Marie Antoinette, especially when chewing on a root they had just dug up with their fingers.

In a few centuries, powdered wigs

It took a long time to make a Frank into a Frenchman, but it was probably worth it.

THE PIPPINS AND CLOVIS

The early Frankish kings were almost all named Pippin. Despite their military prowess, most of them were killed so

[1] These are French Franks, not to be confused with Swiss Franks and German Marks.

early in life that there was no need for old-age pensions. This was especially true of Pippin the Brief.

One king who was famous, though not a Pippin, was Clovis. It is said that when his soldiers were killed in battle, they were buried fully armed. This saved Clovis time, but subsequently blunted the plow of many a French farmer. The most notable thing about Clovis was that he became a Christian. His wife suggested that this would give him an additional reason for fighting neighboring tribesmen, who were heathens.

CHARLES MARTEL

With Charles Martel, history took a Memorable Turn. Henceforth, for hundreds of years, the kings of France were named only Charles. Nothing of equal importance happened until the French discovered the name Louis.

Charles Martel ("The Hammer") was a great warrior although inclined to fly off the handle. As his nickname indicates, he preferred a hammer to a sword, and portraits show him astride a horse, his mighty right arm lifted, about to nail an enemy chieftain.

Charles Martel

In his greatest battle, Charles Martel struck a Decisive Blow that saved Europe from the Mohammedans and caused them to fold their tents and zip up their burnooses. Western civilization was spared unspeakable and unpronounceable horrors. But for Charles Martel's victory, there might now be a Koran in every hotel room.

The greatest of the Frankish kings was Charles the Great, who because of his long hair and flowing beard was called Charles le Mane, later Charlemagne. He was a seven-foot giant of a man under whom the Frankish state reached its height.

For forty years Charlemagne was incessantly engaged in one military conflict or another. In the excitement of combat, his eyes gleamed and his hands shook, causing him to spill blood wherever he went. A shrewd tactician, Charlemagne discovered that all anyone needed to win battles was a larger and stronger army than the opposition, a basic principle of warfare apparently never hit upon by his enemies.

Of the neighboring tribes, the most troublesome to Charlemagne were the Saxons. No matter how often he subjugated them, they remained as revolting as ever.

Charlemagne, we should not forget, was a religious zealot. Often he would pursue his foes relentlessly until their backs were against a river, and then give them the choice of being baptized or drowned. He set many new records for conversion.

CHARLEMAGNE: ADMINISTRATOR AND EDUCATOR

There were no taxes during Charlemagne's reign. Instead, the nobles and wealthy landowners supported the government by their gifts. To make sure the nobles were sufficiently generous, Charlemagne sent forth armed messengers. These went out in pairs so that each could check on the other. In addition, Charlemagne himself was constantly on the road, checking on his messengers. Generous gifts continued to pour in.

A patron of the arts as well as of the bazaars, Charlemagne encouraged learning among the young people of his realm. Unfortunately, he was so busy seeing everyone else off to school that he never learned to write.[1]

CHARLEMAGNE BECOMES EMPEROR

Charlemagne generally got along well with the Pope. He did feel, though, that it was the Pope's job to pray while he, Charlemagne, ran the government.

[1] He could read, however, which put him one up on Mohammed.

The only clash between them occurred on Christmas Day. Charlemagne was opening his presents when the Pope came up from behind and unexpectedly crowned him. When Charlemagne came to, he found he was Emperor of the Romans, although he still felt terribly Teutonic for several days.

A Christmas surprise

THE END OF CHARLEMAGNE'S EMPIRE

Having welded his people and cemented friendships, this great leader thought his realm should last. But disintegration of Charlemagne's empire began soon after his death, by which time he was beginning to go to pieces himself. None of his sons or grandsons had as much character as Charlemagne, and Charles the Bald didn't have as much hair. The empire steadily weakened, and under Charles the Fat it collapsed.

Charlemagne made one significant contribution to Western civilization. He left his foot to measure twelve inches with. He wanted to be remembered as a ruler.

CHAPTER VIII

THE NORSEMEN AND/OR VIKINGS

WE SHOULD NOT forget the Norsemen. But for them, we would probably not have Norway, Sweden, Denmark, Wisconsin, or *smörgåsbord*. These Norsemen were heavily bearded, and tusks grew out of their helmets. They carried an ax in one hand and a spear in the other, which made handshaking impractical. It is generally conceded that the Norsemen looked fierce, and looks were seldom deceiving in those days.

The more adventurous of the Norsemen were known as Vikings, most of whom ran away and joined the Navy at an early age. In their quaint sailing vessels, called *sagas*, they roamed the seas to the south. On one of these voyages they discovered, to their amazement, that not all women are blondes.

The Norsemen's Discovery

Sailing up rivers on boats and traveling inland on horses, the Vikings visited many lands. Something was rotten in the state of Denmark, and they were glad to get away for a change of air. One who stayed home, a bad egg named Omelet, grew so depressed by the Mess in Copenhagen that he became known as the Melancholy Dane. Things got so bad that he began to make long, unintelligible speeches to himself. He also talked to ghosts and skulls and stabbed people in the arras.

The Vikings carried their lack of civilization to many parts of Europe. A few, who were considered extremists, went as far as Russia. One Viking who settled there became known as Eric the Red. Since they were unable to write, they left their mark everywhere, especially on monasteries and churches. They thought the torch was mightier than the pen.

CONQUEST OF ENGLAND

The Vikings started out as plunderers, but, being quick to learn, in almost no time became conquerors. One of the countries they were determined to conquer was England, which was ruled by Edward the Confessor, a garrulous old man who was unable to keep his troubles to himself. For a while they managed to put one of their own people, King Canute, on the throne, but he spent most of his time at the beach, sitting with his feet in the water and wondering what the wild waves were saying. He was unquestionably a Weak Monarch, and a little sandy and damp as well.

King Canute

Despite their introduction of Danish pastry and other colorful Scandinavian customs, the Vikings received a bad press in the *Anglo-Saxon Chronicle*. This caused them to withdraw from England in a huff and several hundred open boats. Crossing the Channel to Normandy, they bided their time until they had produced William the Conqueror.[1]

William met Harold, the English king, at Hastings. It was their first meeting, and they took an immediate dislike to one another. Besides, it was 1066, one of the Significant Dates of

[1] Known as William the Bastard until he became a success.

*Not a moment
to lose*

history, and there wasn't a moment to lose. William seized the opportunity, the throne, and Harold. In this way the Vikings, disguised as Normans, took over England, and proved that perseverance pays.

AFTER-LIFE OF THE VIKINGS

When they died, the Vikings were buried ship and all, whence we derive the expression, "going down with the ship." Some went to Helsinki and others to Valhalla. Valhalla was somewhat more popular, despite the presence of Valkyries, overweight ladies with flaxen braids and huge lungs chock-full of Wagner arias. When they sang, the Valkyries opened their mouths wide and clasped their arms to their breasts, which were heaving. So, by this time, were some of the Vikings.

Entertainment in Valhalla

CHAPTER IX

THE FEUDAL SYSTEM

TO UNDERSTAND the Middle Ages, it is necessary to understand the feudal system, and vice versa. This takes a good deal of patience and an enormous amount of understanding.

After the crumbling of Charlemagne's empire, each of the little crumbs was ruled by a prince. No love was lost, or found, among these rival rulers, and many years of feuding led eventually to feudalism. What had begun as a display of temper became a system.

SOCIAL CLASSES

Everyone was put into a class as soon as he was born, and told to stay there. People in the same class rubbed shoulders, to say nothing of elbows, year after year, and this resulted in frayed clothing and a Static Society.

At the top of the social order were the feudal lords, who lorded it over everybody. They inherited their position, which was usually reclining. Unlike modern society, where it is necessary to know the right people if you want to get to the top, in the Middle Ages you had to be on the right family tree. Otherwise you were simply out on a limb.

The feudal system

Just below the feudal lords were the freemen, so called because they were free to do anything they wanted, as long as the lord permitted it. They were naturally jealous of their freedom and wished they had it.

The serfs were the foundation of feudal society; that is, everyone else was on top of them. Around their necks one end of the chain of command was fastened. But the serfs got some satisfaction out of knowing that a lord was the vassal of a knight who was the vassal of a count or duke who was the vassal of the king.[1] The king, who was nobody's vassal, was usually insane because of inbreeding. Unlike the peasantry, the royal family considered breeding out-of-doors immodest and uncomfortable.

THE MANOR

The economic unit of feudalism was the manor. All of the nobles had manors, but not necessarily good ones. The finest, of course, were those owned by the fealty rich.

A typical manor consisted of the following:

1. *The manor house*, an arrow-proof building located on top of a hill so that the lord of the manor, who looked down on everyone, could keep an eye out for peasants who leaned on their hoes.

2. *The village*. This consisted of peasants' homes, which were without plumbing. This was also true of the manor house, but the manor house was on higher ground. Even the smallest houses had still smaller houses out in back, in which parchment pages were the rough equivalent of a mail-order catalogue.

3. *Peasants' land*. These were very small parcels, neatly wrapped and about one furrow wide. A peasant who couldn't plow straight was often forced to take a one-stroke penalty for going out of bounds.

4. *Common pasturage*. Beyond the village was a place where the peasants met on equal footing with the lord of the manor (when the latter wasn't on horseback). Here also the cattle of all classes grazed without social distinction. The sheep were not

[1] It was a man's world. Woman was known as the weaker vassal.

yet separated from the goats, and papal bulls mingled with the common herd. Some consider this the beginning of democracy.

Since each of the nobles owned his own court and pocketed the fines, peasants were tried as often as possible. When an offender was penniless, he was given a trial by ordeal, which saved the cost of a jury. The most popular ordeals were walking on live brands,[1] carrying a piece of red-hot iron till it cooled, and being thrown into the river. The last two ordeals were never administered together, lest the iron cool prematurely.

Anyone planning a life of crime was well advised to toughen up his hands and feet and learn to swim under water. Even so, first-degree murder often resulted in third-degree burns, and habitual offenders carried bathing caps.

———◆———

CHAPTER X

THE AGE OF CHIVALRY

CHIVALRY WAS a system whereby you pledged yourself to do good deeds, even when you didn't feel in the mood. One advantage over the Boy Scouts was that instead of helping old ladies you helped young ladies, and you got more out of it than a feeble pat on the back. Another advantage was that, although there were dragons, there were no Scoutmasters.

A young man was first a page, then a squire, and finally, after carrying messages for several years, a knight-errand. At this time the king called him in and asked him to kneel so he could get at his shoulder. The king then took a royal stance and a full swing and dubbed him. (He sometimes had a tendency to slice, which he regretted, as did the knight.) As soon as the ceremony was over, the knight picked himself up and went out looking for a damsel to distress.

[1] Not the popular brands.

Becoming a knight

In accordance with the code of chivalry, a knight devoted much of his career to being polite. He was always rushing ahead to pull down drawbridges for fair ladies or to open doors, usually to bedrooms. Now and then he would pick up the handkerchief of a lady who was being eaten by a dragon.

KNIGHT LIFE

Knights were clad in armor which they left outside their door every night to be shined. Armor was a little hard to get in and out of, especially when somebody had borrowed your screwdriver, and only the more fastidious knights bothered to change for dinner. Anyhow, they were in stiff shirts already. Creaking around in armor all day long, a knight found it difficult to distinguish between arthritis and rusty hinges.

When a knight pulled his visor down, he looked just like all the others. To keep the ladies from making embarrassing mistakes, he usually made love with his visor up.

Because of the weight of his armor, a knight preferred riding to walking. What the horse preferred was never ascertained. Mounting was accomplished by means of block and tackle; dismounting was usually taken care of by another knight with a spear.

In addition to his various weapons, a knight carried ladies' gloves, sleeves, and other bits of clothing that had been left

A knight and his weapons

around on purpose.[1] When he was engaged in combat, there was always a beautiful princess leaning over the rampart to encourage him. She did this by dropping roses, handkerchiefs, and, if he looked up at her suddenly, her eyes. Ladies would sometimes faint on seeing their knight run through with a spear, but regain consciousness in time to size up the winner.

Knightly activity

Favorite occupations of the knights were tilting (sometimes they overdid it and fell off), eating, and making love to the queen. Tilting was done in tournaments, where there were long lists of knights who were horsed, unhorsed, or just horsing around. Eating was done in the banquet hall or on a trestle. Making love was done in the king's absence. It was about the only thing a knight didn't do on a horse.

[1] In the Middle Ages, there were no unmentionables worth mentioning.

THE ROUND TABLE

In England, all the knights sat at a round table where King Arthur could watch them if they tried any funny stuff with Queen Guinevere. King Arthur was the inventor of the Round Table discussion, in which the talk went around and around without reaching a conclusion. Among those who took part were Sir Lance a Lot, Sir Gallop Ahead, and the Green Knight— horseback riding made him sick. King Arthur's death came at the hands of a knight who was a square peg in the Round Table. Arthur didn't die a natural death, he was Mordred.

THE MONKS

While the knights went to church on Sunday, the monks stayed there throughout the week. They were confined to cells, although they had done nothing wrong, and all of them had a tendency to get bald in exactly the same place. They were fortunate in being able to copy books without being accused of plagiarism, and could illuminate them if they wanted to read at night. They also had complete medical care and could have their tonsures removed free.

A monk

One of the best things about being a monk was that you could slop around all day in your bathrobe.

During this period, anybody who was anybody went on Crusades. These left every few years, and anyone who was late for one Crusade could usually make the next one. Some scholars, inclined toward cynicism, maintain that the Crusaders left home to get away from their wives and children.

The best-known Crusader was Richard the Lion-Hearted. He is memorable not only for the size of his heart but because he stayed away so long that he became one of the most popular kings of England.

A Crusader

The craze for Crusades ultimately died out, along with most of the Crusaders. Now and then someone today is said to have the Crusading Spirit. It may move him to write a letter to the editor, but it is not likely to move him any farther.

CHAPTER XI

MONGOLS AND OTTOMAN TURKS

JUST WHEN it looked as if there were no more barbarians, the Mongols and Turks turned up. Sympathetic historians say they were not barbarians but westbound Crusaders.

The Mongols were a sturdy people who for thousands of

years had been going up and down the steppes of Asia. Led by Genghis Khan, they swept across Europe, turning fertile fields into deserts and making other significant changes in the agricultural system.

Genghis Khan had a stringy mustache that hung down both corners of his mouth and gave him a sad look. Despite a large collection of concubines, called the Golden Horde, Genghis was an outdoor man and preferred battle.

Every morning he rose early and tried to conquer a few hundred square miles before breakfast. His shock troops went ahead of him and gave everyone a rude surprise. Now and then the Khan grew impatient with progress and boxed his generals' ears. He also boxed the ears of Christians and mailed them home so that the folks would know how he was doing.

Almost as spectacular were the Ottoman Turks, who traveled westward in peculiar shoes with long, curled-up points which

An Ottoman Turk

were comfortable only on the occasional person who had but one toe. The Turks loved beautiful women, and therefore forced their wives to wear veils.[1] They themselves wore fezzes and baggy pants and always seemed on their way to a Shriners' convention.

---

[1] We owe to the Turks the principle that a woman looks better the more she has on, provided a man has a lively imagination.

After getting as far west as Constantinople, the Turks settled down. They were tired of travel and mindful of the old Turkish proverb, "A rolling stone gathers no mosque."

———◆———

CHAPTER XII

FRANCE IN THE MIDDLE AGES

THE FRENCH, who were at first Gauls, then Romans, and then Germans, took their time about becoming French. One of the things that held them back, and caused them to be divided into Elementary, Intermediate, and Advanced, was pronunciation of the "r," which is still impossible for anyone not a native.[1] Some who failed in the classroom have accidentally succeeded in the bathroom, while gargling.

The French way of life was slow in developing. Until there were streets, there could be no streetwalkers. Until there were sidewalks, there could be no sidewalk cafés. Until there were cans, there could be no can-cans.

In time, however, the French character emerged,[2] hastened by the invention of the corkscrew and the beret. In a few hundred years the French were as French as they could get, and had enough Heroic Past to make up for the present.

HUGH CAPET

The first truly French king was Hugh Capet, who no sooner ascended the throne than he became exceedingly dynastic and full of primogeniture. He told the queen that she must have a child at once, and that it must be a son or else. He was always carrying on, and he wanted someone to carry on after him.

It was Hugh Capet who tried uniting Champagne, Burgundy, and Bourbon. He died shortly thereafter.

[1] Not every native can do it, for example the Australian bushman.

[2] It emerged most clearly, and may be seen in the best light, at the Folies Bergère.

THE HUNDRED YEARS' WAR

The Hundred Years' War was a war of succession—a succession of small wars, interspersed with rest periods. It began when the heirs of the house of Capet, who had been dying indoors, died out.

JOAN OF ARK

Joan of Ark, who traced her ancestry back to Noah, was a pleasant girl who heard voices. The voices came out of places where there were no people, which was considered unusual before the invention of the radio. The girl was a good listener, and in a short time had picked up enough knowledge of military tactics to lead the French Army.

Joan was a tender virgin among thousands of rough, hardened troops, but played it safe by never taking off her suit of armor. Astride her horse, carrying a large banner, she was a striking figure, and since she was a woman, no gentleman would strike back.

A Turning Point came when Joan forced the English to lift the siege of the city of Orléans. Joan became popular overnight. Her name was on every tongue, as could be clearly seen when people stood around in open-mouthed amazement.

Joan of Ark

For a time all went well. The French throne was safely in the hands, or under the seat, of Charles VII. Everyone was assured of employment because of the enormous demand for statues and tapestries of Joan. But the poor girl was captured by the English and burnt at the stake. Afterwards they said they were deucedly sorry and all that sort of thing, but it was too little and too late.

The burning of Joan of Ark kindled indignation throughout France, and the French fought as they had never fought before. The English, who were getting very little good out of it, except material for historical novels, decided to leave. A hundred years was long enough for a man to be away from home. Besides, they had to get back to take part in the War of the Roses, which could hardly be fought while the flower of England was in France.

SECOND TEST

1. Do you think Charles Martel ("The Hammer") ever hit his thumb?

2. Discuss the difference between:
   (*a*) Subjugating a Saxon warrior
   (*b*) Conjugating a Saxon verb

3. If Charlemagne was seven times longer than his foot, how long was his arm?

4. "We should not forget the Norsemen." Point out the fallacies in this statement.

5. Which did the Valkyries fear most:
   (*a*) Wotan?
   (*b*) Siegfried?
   (*c*) Laryngitis?

6. What happened to a feudal lord when he was caught with his drawbridge down?

7. Define the word "fief." (It is *not* the number between four and six.)

8. How far can you carry a red-hot iron? Don't you think this is carrying it a little too far?

9. What was the queen doing while the king was in the counting house? Did he ever fool her by counting by tens? Was this chivalrous?

10. When did the French learn about good wine years and bad wine years? How often have you tried to impress your friends with this sort of thing?

CHAPTER XIII

MEDIEVAL LEARNING AND LITERATURE

DURING THE Dark Ages, everyone was ignorant. Toward the end of the Middle Ages, someone threw the switch and there was a Revival of Learning. Revival meetings were held throughout France and Italy. People began to know more and more, and to correct each other on names and dates and the source of familiar quotations. Universities opened their doors; those that taught chemistry opened their windows. The first university was named Bologna, probably by the students.

One of the leading scholars was Tom S. Aquinas. Those who believed his theories were known as Tomists; those who weren't quite sure were called Doubting Tomists. Superficial students, who only skimmed his works, were referred to as Peeping Tomists. There was also Abelard, who taught Peripatetics. He gave a correspondence course to a girl named Hello Louise, who is thought to have been one of the early telephone operators. Abelard, who was frail and dialectic, died before his time.[1]

LITERARY ACCOMPLISHMENTS

Most books were written in Latin in order to keep knowledge out of the hands of laymen who might mislay it. Romance languages were used for Belles Lettres, Love Lettres, and Billet Douches.

The greatest writer was Dante, the author of a humorous work called *The Divine Comedy*, in which the hero goes to hell. There was also Boccaccio, who wrote a book full of naughty stories, some of which are printed only in Italian in order to stimulate study of the language.

Chaucer, a family man, was the father of English poetry, even though he could not spell. The most famous line in Chaucer's *Canterbury Tales* is the first, "Whan that Aprille with his shoures soote," because few people ever get past it.

[1] This was customary. Very few people in the Middle Ages died after their time.

Chaucerian spelling

Chaucer's best-known character is the Wife of Bath, who despite her name was hardly an example of clean living. Although Chaucer wrote hundreds of years ago, he can be read without difficulty today by anyone who can turn the page while keeping one finger in the glossary.

Most other writers were Anonymous, which made it troublesome for their biographers.

———◆———

CHAPTER XIV

THE GUILDS AND MEDIEVAL TRADE

OF GREAT IMPORTANCE during the Middle Ages were the guilds, which supplied labor trouble before the discovery of unions. Their membership consisted of craftsmen, craftswomen, crafty merchants, and a few slick customers. A man began as an apprentice, and after a few years was permitted to travel about as a journeyman, with an expense account. Ultimately he became a master, or even a Jack of All Trades.[1]

Guilds engaged in many enterprises. One of these was guilding lilies. Another was sponsoring fairs and fair trade. The Theater

[1] The Jack was ranked just under the King and Queen.

Guild put on miracle plays, so called because they kept showing for years and years despite bad reviews.

Europeans had a craving for spices. Without spices, food was tasteless. Many brave young men were sent to the Orient for seasoning.

Europeans loved spices

Mostly, however, spices were brought from Asia by traders who came by one or more of the following means:

1. Caravans
2. Trade routes
3. Trade winds
4. Camels
5. Luckies

In the caravans, along with traders, were exotic dancing girls [1] clad in as many as seven veils. As they warmed up, they removed the veils one at a time, until they were comfortable. After meals their dancing wafted delicate perfume about and helped remove the odor of fried camel. Meantime background music of lutes and flutes and throbbing drums drowned out the groans and belches of those who had overeaten.

Some of the spice traders were sheiks, but because of scraggly beards and stained teeth they bore little resemblance to

[1] Not ballet but belly dancers.

Rudolph Valentino. A sheik and his party were never seated behind a tent pole but always given a table at the edge of the dance floor. Dancing girls would sometimes do a routine up close for those who were nearsighted. With almost impossible impassiveness, the sheik remained unmoved. But afterwards he was likely to turn up at the stage entrance with a box of figs and ask for a date.

What with feasting, floor shows, and sandstorms, caravans were often behind schedule in getting from East to West. Meanwhile Europeans, timetables in hand, impatiently awaited the arrival of spice traders, prepared to welcome them with open salt and pepper shakers.

THE RISE OF CITIES

Cities were growing increasingly important, especially to mayors and aldermen. Unfortunately, many cities were ruled by despots, tosspots, and other unscrupulous persons. Startling revelations were contained in books like *Casbah Confidential* and *Inside Oudh*. Men began to be civic-minded in order to have an excuse to get out of the house one or two nights a week.

A word about Hamelin, a city that became celebrated for its Ratskeller, a rodent-infested beer garden where the Piper got Pied. A word also about Venice, where canals were ingeniously substituted for streets, thus drastically reducing paving costs.

Cities were rising. So were citizens, although later than when they lived on the farm.

CHAPTER XV

SWITZERLAND BECOMES A NATION

AT FIRST Switzerland was not a nation but just a lot of Swiss, who were too busy eking out a living to exclaim about the view. If they occasionally looked up at the Alps, it was only to see whether an avalanche was starting. In this land of cliffs and crevasses, it was marginal living.

To make their lives harder, they were dominated by Austria. The Swiss, a proud people who knew that they alone could grow edelweiss, looked down on the Austrians. The Austrians, in turn, thought the Swiss had the wrong altitude, and did everything they could to break their spirit. But the Swiss, the inventors of Swiss steak, were too tough for them.

The hero of Switzerland was a gossipy fellow named William Tell, who made an impassioned appeal to Austria, known as William Tell's Overture. Failing in this, he rallied his people with the stirring cry, "An apple a day keeps the Austrians away." His son, Flathead Tell, dramatized this concept by standing for hours in the public square, fearlessly balancing an apple on his head. A somewhat erratic archer, William Tell aimed at his son and shot an arrow through the heart of Schiller, the Austrian tyrant, a thoroughly bad apple who was rotten to the core.

William Tell & Son

Once rid of the Austrians, the Swiss moved into resort towns and barricaded themselves in hotels for protection against tourists. This mass migration was known as the Swiss Movement. Awaiting the onslaught, the Swiss nervously carved the edges of tables and the backs of chairs into cuckoo clocks. Thus began a Great Industry.

51

Wars have raged all around Switzerland for centuries, but this little country has never been invaded. Stronger nations have been frightened off by the rugged terrain and the possibility of hearing someone yodel. Another deterrent has been the fierce St. Bernard dogs, with casks of brandy tied to their necks, always ready to take a nip.

The scenery of Switzerland is breathtaking, particularly up around 20,000 feet. In their lovely country the Swiss have become prosperous by importing mountain climbers,[1] poking holes in cheese, and manufacturing such sports equipment as skis, ski poles, splints, and crutches. The Swiss are a healthy race, their sanitariums being devoted exclusively to foreigners. Now and then, however, an epidemic of chicken pox leaves a few dotted Swiss. Although clean-living, the Swiss are not always clean-shaven, perhaps because their shaving brushes are used as ornaments on their hats.

———◆———

CHAPTER XVI

THE RENAISSANCE

THE MIDDLE AGES had no sooner come to an end than the Renaissance got under way. Everybody was reborn. New vistas were opened up and old vistas were renovated. The inquiring spirit was everywhere, and the mark of the age was the question mark.

REBIRTH OF ART

Everyone was either a painter or sculptor or both, and museums were beginning to fill up. The Old Masters were still young and had even younger models, whom they painted without any clothes on. On chilly days they painted bowls of fruit

[1] Business has fallen off somewhat since the discovery of the Himalayas.

and vases of flowers, or, if they were of the realistic school, portraits of their wives.

The favorite subject of most artists was themselves. They stood in front of a mirror and unflinchingly painted what they saw. By painting their own portraits, they not only saved money but took no chances on what other artists might do to them.

The self-portrait

Among the famous artists was Titian, who painted nudes on a large scale. He liked quantity more than quality. He also liked his models to have red hair and flesh-colored flesh and to hold still. Another artist was Leonardo da Vinci, who painted Mona Lisa. It tickled Mona to be painted, and she had a hard time keeping a straight face. It was da Vinci, we might add, who invented the first airplane and had enough sense not to fly in it. Finally there was Michelangelo, who painted until he filled all the walls and had to paint on his back. Michelangelo was also a sculptor, probably the greatest chiseler of his time.

ADVANCE OF SCIENCE

This was a period of great scientific discoveries and important inventions. Results may be summarized as follows:

1. Gunpowder made the peasant the equal of the prince, provided his hand didn't shake too much.

Equality

2. The lens led to the microscope, the telescope, the periscope, the horoscope,[1] the optometrist, and bifocals.

3. Arabic numerals made it easier to divide 48 by 8 than XLVIII by VIII, and looked better on class sweaters.

4. Movable type was a convenience for printers who liked to travel.

5. The mariner's compass made sailors feel less at sea.

6. The discovery that the earth revolves around the sun, instead of the sun around the earth, caused resentment on the part of those who took it personally.

THE MEDICI

During the Renaissance, almost every artist had a patron, *i.e.*, a wealthy man who, instead of buying an artist's works, bought the artist. The artist was given his room and board in return for painting flattering portraits of the family in which he uncrossed eyes, overlooked double chins, and made it easier for patricians to look down their noses.

Of all the patrons, the most patronizing were the Medici, the best known of whom were Cosimo, Lorenzo, and Religio. One of the friends of the Medici was Machiavelli, inventor of the double-cross, which eventually proved more effective than

[1] The scope of things to come.

*Machiavelli
and friend*

either the right cross or the left hook. A disagreeable sort, he believed the end justified being mean. A French contemporary of the Medici was Rabelais. Ladies left the room when he told his stories, but later read them in his Collected Works.

———◆———

CHAPTER XVII

EXPLORATIONS

ONE OF THE things that kept people busy during the Renaissance was pushing back the horizon, which had long been too close for comfort. Thanks to the efforts of various Intrepid Explorers, it was moved to approximately its present position.

Explorers usually spent several years going from court to court in search of supporters, meanwhile holding up their pants as best they could. Now and then a king would give them a belt and send them on their way. A good subject for debate was whether the earth was round, but it was hard to find people to take the affirmative.

There were, in general, three kinds of explorers:

1. Those who left a dotted line behind them.
2. Those who left a solid line behind them.
3. Those who left their loved ones behind them.

MARCO POLO

One of the earliest explorers was Marco Polo, a young Venetian. At an age when most of his playmates were begging their parents to let them take out the family gondola, young Marco was on his way to China. His travels took him through many strange lands, including Terra Incognita, where everyone went around under an assumed name. He wrote home regularly, and asked that the envelopes be saved for his stamp collection.

According to his own story, Marco Polo made an immense hit with the Chinese emperor and learned four languages in a few days. He told the emperor such fascinating tales of his travels that he was given an important governmental position, probably making up accounts. The emperor had a serious surplus problem—too many wives—and wanted Marco Polo to stay on and help him through the crisis. But Marco, a Venetian at heart, was getting homesick for glass blowing and spaghetti sucking, and took his leave. A sentimental fellow, he also took a

Marco grew homesick

huge cargo of spices and precious stones to remember the emperor by.

Marco Polo eventually reached home, smelling of spices and with enough material for a book. This was published under the title of *So You're Going to the Orient,* and contained helpful hints about what to take, how much to tip, and the correct manner of wiping chopsticks on your pants. Marco Polo lived to a fairly ripe old age and left a large number of descendants, known as Marco's Millions.

CHRISTOPHER COLUMBUS

Christopher Columbus is notorious for discovering America. But, while this is discussed in detail in many books, little is said of what compelled him to leave Europe. No explanation is given for the confused and distracted state of mind that caused him to go west when he wanted to reach the East. What made him tell Ferdinand and Isabella that an egg was round instead of egg-shaped? Why did he spend seventy days at sea? Who else ever mistook Cuba for Japan? Why did he carry a pistol and mutter to himself about "dead reckoning"?

Obviously, we need to know more about the Early Years. Columbus was born in Italy and later in Spain, taught himself Latin in a one-pupil schoolhouse, and didn't run away at an early age. Facts are meager, perhaps cunningly hidden by the Columbus family, but various clues lead us to the following conjectures:

1. Columbus was in some sort of trouble, even before he set sail. Why else would he have changed his name from Columbo to Columbus and then to Colon?

2. There was more between Columbus and Queen Isabella than just King Ferdinand.

3. He was plagued by financial difficulties, as indicated by his failure, even after discovery of the New World, to get credit.

4. He had three wives, which was an odd number. Histories of the period give us little information about these women except that they were named María, Pinta, and Niña. The last

was the smallest, but the most difficult. It took twenty-two men to manage her. When she left for America with Columbus she was loaded.

MAGELLAN

It was Ferdinand Magellan, a Portuguese navigator, who first discovered a route around the world and thereby made himself indispensable in crossword puzzles and geography tests.

His famous voyage took him around South America and, one calm day, into the ocean he promptly named the Pacific. He later hit some nasty weather, but it was too late to give the ocean another name. When his men wanted to turn back, he said he would push on, even if he had to eat the leather of the rigging. They stayed with him, thinking it would be a sight worth waiting for.

Magellan's greatest achievement was proving that the earth was round. After sailing for thirty-six months, every day thinking he was about to drop off the edge of the earth, he dropped anchor instead, exactly where he started from. Cynics maintained that he might just as well never have left.

———◆———

CHAPTER XVIII

EUROPE ON THE EVE OF MODERN TIMES

EUROPE WAS now on the eve of modern times. Everybody was excited and could hardly wait.

Modern times were ushered in by wars and rumors of war, most of the latter being well founded. In England there was a struggle between the Tudors and the Fourdors that led eventually to the station wagon. In Spain an outburst of inquisitiveness brought on the Spanish Inquisition. In France the king wanted to enlarge his realm, in which there was no room to build a new palace. He looked covetously at the Italian boot, and before long had put his foot into it.

The Thirty Years' War lasted so long that the combatants became known as the Lost Generation, thus comparing favorably with the Lost Battalions of other wars. It was a religious war, fought to see which side was more religious, and seldom has there been so much piety on the field of battle. There were constant attacks and counter-attacks, Reformations and Counter-Reformations. The war took an unusual turn with the entry of the King of Denmark, who was a Holstein, and Gustavus Adolphus of Sweden, the Lion of the North. They fought with animal fury. Gustavus fell in the heat of battle, being unaccustomed to the southern climate. At length[1] the war ended with the Peace of Westfailure. It was an uneasy peace, as usual.

THE HAPSBURGS

Germany, meanwhile, was under the rule of the Hapsburg family, whose distinguishing feature was the Hapsburg lip.

The Hapsburg lip

No Hapsburg was without one. As soon as a Hapsburg was born, his lower lip was carefully examined and measured with a yardstick. If it failed to come up to expectations or down to his chin, in other words wasn't king-size, the little Hapsburg was declared ineligible. Many courtiers, engaged as specialists, gave only lip service.

[1] But seventy years short of a tie for the longest war.

The most memorable Hapsburgs were:

1. Rudolph the Red-Nosed Hapsburg, who lived in a castle atop a remote mountain and discouraged door-to-door salesmen.

2. Maxie Million I, known as "The Fixer," who arranged marriages between, and sometimes behind, royal houses. He kept a little black book full of the names of women with attractive dowries.

3. Charles V, who surrounded himself with artists and thus could be seen only in portraits, which was a Good Thing.

4. Francis Joseph, whose bushy sidewhiskers started a fad and, among cigar smokers, some dangerous brush fires.

CHAPTER XIX

REVOLT OF THE NETHERLANDS

FOR A LONG time the Netherlands was under the heel of Spain, who was Philip II. But Philip refused to live there, preferring to stay in Spain, where he ruled in Absentia, a small town on the coast. Philip was cold and enigmatic, and his doctor advised him to stay in a warm climate.

Philip II

The most ill-advised act of Philip was sending the Duke of Alva to be regent in the Netherlands. Alva was high-handed and low-principled, and the spirits of the Netherlanders fell so far that their land became known as the Low Country.

Fortunately for the Netherlanders, a hero arose in their mist. He was a jaundiced gentleman known as William the Orange. His rallying cries inspired even the Flemish, a slow-spoken people who were always clearing their throats.

Victory over Philip came when the Netherlanders opened a hole in the Dike and drowned the enemy. They stationed a boy at the Dike who put his finger in the hole as soon as the last Spaniard was good and soggy. After the war, there was a celebration that lasted for weeks. Finally someone remembered the boy, still holding his finger in the hole. They did the only decent thing and erected a statue of him.

Van Dike

CONTRIBUTIONS OF THE NETHERLANDS

Although a small country, the Netherlands has left its mark on European culture. Consider for a moment, or even longer, its contribution to art. It is the home of Rembrandt, whose "Night Watch" is celebrated for its luminous dial; of Van Dike,[1] who sneaked through galleries, painting mustaches and

[1] Not related to the one that sprang a leak.

beards on pictures of women; and of Van Go, the restless genius known as the Moving Van.

Its cheese has made itself smelt throughout Europe. Its windmills, which draw water from the ground and tourists from all over the world, have contributed two new words to our own vocabulary—"picturesque" and "quaint."

The Dutch are a sensible people. They grow tulips for the bulbs, which don't wilt the way the blossoms do. They trustingly leave their wooden shoes on the doorstep, knowing they can hear anyone walking off in them. And they are the inventors of the Dutch Treat, which is a Good Idea.

The chief city of this interesting little country is Amsterdam, known as "the Venice of the North." By reciprocal arrangement, Venice is called "the Amsterdam of the South."

PRACTICE PROJECTS

1. Demonstrate the sort of artificial respiration used in a Greek Revival.

2. Go to the zoo and get a whiff of a camel. Now do you see why the medieval traders carried spices?

3. Draw a resource map of Switzerland, crosshatching the areas richest in edelweiss and yodelers.

4. Go to an art gallery and look at a reproduction. (For students over 16.)

5. Box a compass. Don't worry, it won't hit back.

6. Look at yourself in the mirror. If you resemble a Hapsburg, visit a genealogist and have your background examined.

7. Make a list of the things Magellan would have eaten after he finished the leather on the rigging.

8. With your mind fixed on the little Dutch boy and the dike, stick your finger up a faucet and turn the water on full force. Comment. Or if you speak French, *"Comment?"*

CHAPTER XX

LOUIS XIV

LOUIS XIV RULED France by Divine Right, which gave him a sense of security. The job was his as long as he wanted it. Another nice thing was always being right. No one in the palace ever thought of correcting him on a name or date. His pencils had no erasers.

Louis was known as the Sun King and had no objection. He rather liked the sun, except that he thought it rose too early. He himself stayed in bed until noon, but told anyone who had business with him in the morning to come on up. He always wore his wig and his best nightgown.

Few kings have lived in such luxury or in so many palaces. Among his many estates were Versailles and a windy spot called Fountainblow. He was proudest of Versailles, which had as many rooms as a hotel, all of them royal suites. It was full of echoing corridors where the king's wisecracks were repeated over and over, much to his satisfaction. Louis was surrounded by courtiers and, in the Hall of Mirrors, by himself.

Louis was in many ways a Grand Monarch. For instance, he encouraged writers and artists, many of whom were terribly discouraged. Writers like Racine gave French literature a certain raciness, and Molière brought the French stage to its height, which unfortunately was above the heads of his audience. The king graciously came to the assistance of Madame de Sévigné, the leading letter writer of the day, by letting her use the royal box at the post office.

LOUIS HAS DIFFICULTIES

But Louis also had his troubles. He sometimes got caught in the trappings of royalty and had to call for help. Then too, the drafty corridors of Fountainblow gave him the sniffles, and he frequently sneezed into his snuffbox. Worst of all, he confused strangers and annoyed friends by saying "I am the State" when

Louis was always right

he was really Louis. He could hardly have expected to fool anyone for long.

What with new wings for Versailles and new wigs for himself, Louis lived extravagantly. He always had an idea for spending money up his sleeve, along with half a dozen lace handkerchiefs. Colbert, his Finance Minister, was a Hard Money man, and was forever pleading with him to keep his old wig and his old mistress a few weeks longer. But when Colbert asked, "Where's the money to come from?" Louis had a stock answer: "The people." Divine Right wasn't much good if it didn't take care of the upkeep.

Although Louis was an absolute monarch,[1] he accepted help from a group of advisers known as the Privy Council. These men sat in a small building in back of Versailles and came to some important conclusions.

The power behind the throne

MADAME DE MAINTENON

Louis married the daughter of the King of Spain, but shortly afterward began having a succession of mistresses, known as the Spanish Succession. One of these mistresses was Madame de Maintenon, who was also the royal governess, charged with segregating the natural from the unnatural children. She did such a good job that Louis finally married her, but kept the

[1] When he wasn't being dissolute.

marriage a secret from his courtiers so they wouldn't think him a prude.

Because he had the gout, Louis had his throne put on wheels and Madame de Maintenon pushed him anywhere he wanted to go.[1] Thus she was acknowledged to be the power behind the throne.

LAST DAYS

Louis outlived almost everyone, including his son and grandson. They are still talking about the Age of Louis XIV.

———◆———

CHAPTER XXI

THE RISE OF RUSSIA

THE EARLY RUSSIANS, who have been called "children of the steppes," or steppe children, lived far to the north, in a cold and forbidding region. By dressing warmly in bearskins and long beards, they managed to live fairly comfortably. Their tastes were simple, and they could exist for months on nothing but caviar, tundra, and Frozen Borscht, which they thawed out on the way down with a vodka chaser.

A fabulous Russian of early times was the Vulgar Boatman, later identified as O. Chichornia, who walked along the shore pulling boats up and down the river. He sang a mournful song over and over while he worked. If he sounded sad, it was because he was at the end of his rope.

There were also the Cossacks, fierce horsemen in shiny leather boots who could dance while sitting down. They usually wore their hats, even indoors, because they didn't expect to stay long.

The Russian rulers, or czars,[2] were all called Ivan or Peter, with the possible exception of Catherine.

[1] He didn't like it when anyone else pushed him around.
[2] Also spelled *tsars*. Probably related to the Russian *czigars* and *tsigarettes*.

67

IVAN THE TERRIBLE

Ivan the Terrible is easier to remember than Ivan IV, although he is the same man. Going beyond his predecessors, who spread only caviar, Ivan spread terror. Before he died he had made a name for himself.

As a boy, he tortured animals. Later he displayed a certain kindness toward bears, to whom he fed people who annoyed him.

Everything about Ivan was terrible—his looks, his manners, his taste, his jokes. At first Ivan resented being called the Terrible, but he gradually got used to it and even came to be proud of his reputation as a perfectionist. "If a thing is worth doing at all," he said, "it is worth doing terribly."

PETER THE GREAT

After Ivan the Terrible there were some fair-to-middling Russian rulers, such as Boris Goodenough. Then came Peter the Great, a tall, strapping fellow. People who got off with no more than a strapping were lucky.

As a young Czar, Peter made the Grand Tour of Europe. He went through museums in Italy, skied in the Alps, saw the sights of Paris, wrote postcards from the Riviera, and floated down the Rhine until pulled out. Peter was impressed. Returning to Russia, his suitcases plastered with hotel stickers, he resolved to make his homeland like Europe so that he could enjoy himself without all the travel.

Peter Europeanized his subjects

One of Peter's first achievements was moving the capital to St. Petersburg. There was something about the name of the place that appealed to him. In his efforts to Europeanize his subjects, Peter unveiled Russian women, cut the beards off his courtiers, and went so far as to remove the head of the Church. When he died, he left Russians veneered with European culture.

CATHERINE THE GREAT

Catherine the Great was a stoutish woman who took Russian expansion seriously and extended her frontiers in all directions.

One of the first things she did was to get rid of her husband, since she found it embarrassing to order the Czar around in front of the servants. Besides, her lovers were beginning to queue up at the door and there was an unnecessary amount of saluting as the Czar went in and out.

Once she had her husband done away with, and had a good cry in public, Catherine was free to concentrate on other affairs. These she had with a large assortment of gentlemen, each of whom she made a general or admiral for his services to the state.

Catherine rewarded her friends

One of her kindest acts was telling the Russian serfs that she was sorry for their lot. She did this just before taking their lots away from them entirely. On the other hand, she failed to say a comforting word when she dismembered Poland.

Catherine frequently entertained literary personages such as Diderot, who complimented her on her mind, a part of her which had been overlooked by most of her friends. He made her think she was a Thinker. Some say Catherine corresponded with Voltaire, but actually the similarity was slight.

———◆———

CHAPTER XXII

FREDERICK THE GREAT

FREDERICK THE GREAT [1] was the great-grandson of Frederick William, the German who invented a way of stuffing ballot boxes and thus became known as the Great Elector. There was a strain of greatness in the family.

Frederick's father, Frederick William I,[2] thought his son would never amount to anything because he preferred playing the flute and writing poetry to killing people. Fortunately for German music and literature, Frederick was persuaded to take up a military career before he had done any harm.

Besides being a German, Frederick was a Hohenzollern and a Prussian. He tried to make up for this by writing essays in French and taking dancing lessons, but it was no use. The Prussian in him kept coming out, and there was always more where that came from. After a while he just let himself go and became a general. Day and night he wore a fancy-dress uniform, liberally covered with military decorations and smudges of metal polish.

A short man with an erect posture, Frederick was most at ease when he was at attention. Whether raising a beer stein or cutting a sausage, he did so with military precision, usually clicking his heels as he wiped the foam off his mustache. But despite his Prussian tendencies, he was known as an Enlightened Despot, especially by those who did not know him well.

After careful inspection to see that there were no buttons

---

[1] Also known, because of certain of his personal habits, as Frederick the Gross.

[2] Frederick William I was the grandson of Frederick William. This sort of thing is hard to explain.

missing,[1] Frederick sent his troops into battle. He always exhorted them to win, or at any rate not to lose the crease in their trousers. Frederick was a shrewd tactician. His cleverest trick was a way he had of Turning Defeat Into Victory, but he refused to tell anyone how he did it. Frederick's greatest success was when he won the Seven Years' War and took the Oder away from Maria Theresa.

This famous king is best remembered for his friendship with Voltaire. He invited Voltaire to be his guest at his summer palace, and they spent many happy days trading insults and toasting each other. Their enduring friendshp was based on the fact that Frederick thought Voltaire immensely clever and so did Voltaire.

Voltaire and Frederick

CHAPTER XXIII

THE AGE OF REASON

WE NOW COME to the Age of Reason, a period when reason was in season. It was a wonderful time in which to live: women were so reasonable that even the workingman could afford a mistress or two.

[1] Frederick inspected his troops with the help of a psychiatrist.

In England, important scientific discoveries were made by men like Sir Isaac Newton, who saw an apple fall from a tree and drew a Grave Conclusion.[1] In France, Lavoisier specialized in the conservation of matter, saving string, old magazines, and empty boxes until he hardly had room to work. In Holland, a Dutchman observed bacteria under his microscope and apologized for not keeping it cleaner. Science was in the saddle, which made experiments difficult but got scientists out in the open.

Everyone had a furrowed brow and a worried look, but was only thinking. Favorite places for thinking were the Parisian saloons, where more ears were bent than elbows. These saloons were usually presided over by Madame Somebody-or-Other, who kept fanning herself furiously in the hope that some gentleman would think her overheated and take her out onto the balcony. She also wore a beauty patch on her cheek, chin, forehead, or wherever it would stick, and managed to hide at least that much of her. Guests who said she looked young and beautiful were invited again.

The beauty patch

DESCARTES

Few thinkers were able to outthink René Descartes, who in a thoughtful moment said, "I think I think and therefore I think

[1] That it was ripe.

I am—I think." The followers of this famous thinker, known as Cartesians, placed their philosopher ahead of all others; in fact went so far as to put Descartes before the horse.

Jean Jacques Rousseau was a sociable philosopher. While scientists were busy in the laboratory, he conducted his experiments in the parlor and bedroom. Few philosophers have given themselves so enthusiastically to their work. Many consider him the founder of the Romantic Movement.

Almost everyone loved Rousseau, except Voltaire, who didn't like the way Rousseau thought, and certain Frenchmen who didn't like the way he looked at their wives. When Rousseau brought out his *Confessions*, a number of important people turned at once to the index.

Above all, Rousseau loved noble savages, unspoiled by running water, marriage, and clothes. He liked simple people, and found a good many of them even in Paris. In order to get away from the pressures of civilization, he sold his watch. This made him relaxed, happy, and usually late.

In his *Social Contract*, Rousseau made such statements as "Man is born free, and everywhere he is in chains." This was the beginning of double talk, later to prove indispensable in government.

———◆———

CHAPTER XXIV

LOUIS XV

IN HIS EARLY years, Louis XV, or Cans, devoted himself to the chase.[1] It was hoped that his marriage would put an end to this unseemly conduct, but it failed to do so. It was Louis XV who coined that memorable French expression, *"Ah, c'est la vie!"*

[1] See his invention of the *chase longue*, for affairs of some duration.

There was something about him that was attractive to women. As his pictures reveal, it was not his face.

The king often had audiences in his closet. This only proves that the audiences couldn't have been very large. It took a great many valets to help Louis up in the morning. The Upper Valet assisted him into his shirt and the Lower Valet assisted him into his trousers. By the time Louis had gone through his wig rack and chosen his hair style for the day, it was usually time to get back into bed.

Louis Cans

Historians consider this Louis a Weak King.

When he wasn't getting dressed or undressed, Louis was usually thinking, most often of himself. Always one to excel, he has been called the Supreme Egotist. No one ever thought more of Louis XV than Louis XV.

TWO MISTRESSES

One of Louis' favorite favorites was Madame de Pompadour, whom the king met at a masked ball. When she took off her mask, she looked even better than before,[1] and the king asked her for a rendezvous.

"*Rendez vous*?" asked King Louis.

[1] Louis, who was the sly sort, kept his mask on for several days.

She did not reply at once, but the king pressed her for an answer. Finally, not wishing to make a scene, she admitted she did, and Louis, who was not yet a Weak King, carried her off to Versailles.

Madame de Pompadour soon had Louis under her thumb. After dinner it was the custom for Louis to wash the dishes while Madame de Pompadour set the fashions of France. She inspired the multiple petticoat, which always had more layers than a wedding cake, and the bustle, which gave the illusion that something was there, even when it wasn't. Her upswept coiffure was widely imitated, and many homely women looked just like Madame de Pompadour from the hairline up.

But after a time Madame de Pompadour fell out of Louis' favor and broke her left clavicord. Happily for Louis, who was badly in need of a new mistress, he met Madame du Barry. The king admired her high spirits and her low-cut dress, and in no time they were bosom friends.

Madame du Barry has been the subject of many paintings, some of

Madame de Pompadour

which are now used on the jackets of hysterical novels. She has been best memorialized, however, in chairs especially designed by Louis XV and famous for their padding in the seat and the graceful curve of their legs.[1]

CHAPTER XXV

LOUIS XVI

UNLIKE LOUIS XV, who gradually became weak, Louis XVI was born that way. He thus got a head start, and easily maintained his lead.

The greatest weakness of Louis XVI was for food. He drank wine by the hogshead and ate hogs by the hog. When a servant asked him, "How many eggs do you want for breakfast, Sire— one or two?" he meant dozen. His excuse for eating so much at a time when so many of his subjects were starving, was that it was cheaper to buy food in quantity. Most of the dandies of the day walked around with a cane, but Louis carried only a toothpick.

One effect of all this eating was that Louis became a rounder. After a heavy lunch, Louis often went to sleep in meetings of the Royal Council, and the only motions he made were stretching and scratching.

But Louis was not weak everywhere, only in the head. He had strong shoulders, which he developed by smashing Louis XV chairs. This not only kept him in good physical condition but led to Louis XVI chairs.

France had been plunged into debt and depression by the excesses of the previous regime, and Louis coined various slogans, such as "a snail in every pail," to cheer the populace. But the people kept crying for reform. What they really wanted was the king's scalp, which they planned to remove at the neck.

[1] Louis XV's furniture was made by the court cabinetmaker, Rococo.

Marie Antoinette, the beautiful daughter of Maria Theresa of Austria, married Louis XVI when he was only a dolphin. It was a marriage of convenience, but it is hard to see why.

Marie Antoinette and Louis XVI

Marie was a gay sort, an incorrigible croquette. She found court life so dull that she had Louis build her a little seventeen-room shack in the woods back of Versailles where she could throw an occasional wild party without disturbing the neighbors. Marie thought of herself as a *femme fatale*, and was always winking at strange men to see whether she could make them swoon. Now and then one fell at her feet, either overcome by her charms or tripped by his sword. When she winked at the unimaginative Louis, he usually whipped out his handkerchief and asked her if she had something in her eye.

Some historians maintain that Marie Antoinette was selfishly concerned with her own pleasures and heedless of the poor. Yet when the crowd at the palace gates cried out for bread, she thought that wasn't good enough for them, and said "Let them eat cake." This not only showed her high regard for the people but won her the undying gratitude of French pastry makers.

CHAPTER XXVI

THE FRENCH REVOLUTION

THE SIGNAL for the French Revolution was the fall of the Bastille, a rickety building that had been condemned. The Old Regime, just down the street, was also tottering. About the only safe place was the Hôtel de Ville, where all the rooms had been reserved for months by Convention delegates. The Convention met to frame the Constitution, but framed the king instead.

The common people were fed up with royalty, but still hungry. A great mob went after the king and found him playing tennis. He was off his game, and what they heard, known as the Tennis Court Oath, convinced them that he was not fit to be

The Tennis-Court Oath

their ruler. They intended only to wash his mouth out with soap, but one thing led to another and they wound up by taking away his tennis racket and his membership card.

Anybody who could tell a cockade from a stockade shouted

"Vive le roi!"

"Vive la république" and "Give us liberty, fraternities, and sororities." A few die-hards, who thought their necks were too tough for the guillotine, shouted *"Vive le roi,"* but they were cut off short.

A climax was reached when an all-male Assembly approved the Declaration of the Rights of Man. This affirmed man as the Stronger Sex and established his right

1. To tell a story without interruption or correction.

2. To come in late without explaining why.

3. To have a Double Standard, which permitted double-crossing and double-dealing.

THE GUILLOTINE

The Radicals now took over, and blood began to flow in all the major arteries. These Radicals were either Sans-culottes (without pants), Girondists, or Jacobins. In those perilous days it was a good idea either to belong to a club or to carry one.

Among the bloodiest leaders of the Revolution were Robespierre, Danton, and Marat. Robespierre inflamed people with his speeches and caused some nasty skin disorders. As a member of the Committee of Public Safety, he conscientiously rid the city of jaywalkers, sleepwalkers, and bird watchers. His wholesale executions kept the price within everyone's reach. As for Danton, his policy was "boldness, more boldness, and even more boldness." He didn't scare easily, perhaps because he never made a public speech until his bodyguards had frisked the audience. Marat was the one who was stabbed by Charlotte Corday while he was taking a bath. Charlotte hated him for the way he used up all the hot water, splashed the floor, and left a ring around the tub.

Charlotte's revenge

The guillotine got to be the center of social life in Paris. Heads and drums were rolling, and there was a general feeling of instability. Now and then somebody took a tumbrel on the cobblestones, and the women, who sat around knitting, laughed themselves into stitches. It was a gruesome sight, and blood was thicker than water.

An interesting sidelight of the Rain of Terror, as this period was called by those who weren't enjoying themselves, was the story of Charles Darnay [1] and Sydney Carton. These two men looked so much alike that the executioner, Old Bailey, cut Sydney's head off by mistake. He was terribly sorry about it afterward and tried to make amends, but unfortunately this was before the invention of Scotch Tape.

[1] Who went under the name of Charles Dickens after he escaped to England.

Clouds were now gathering on the horizon. Louis and Marie were in the royal apartments with the shades drawn and failed to see them. The storm broke, and another Rain of Terror began. The populace, instead of hailing the king and queen, pelted their windows with stones. The royal couple fled from Paris by coach, being unable to afford a Pullman, and almost escaped across the border. While they were going through customs, however, Louis was asked if he had anything to declare. He couldn't resist the opportunity to make a long speech, and this gave his pursuers a chance to overtake them.

After anguishing in prison for a while, the king and queen were brought out and told to take off their hats. The executioner then took off their heads. The crowd applauded, considering this capital punishment.

THE DIRECTORY

France was now ruled by a group of men who, because they had their names in the telephone book, were known as The Directory.

———◆———

CHAPTER XXVII

NAPOLEON

NAPOLEON WAS BORN in Corsica in straightened circumstances, which accounts for his fine posture. Little is known of his parents, except that he has been referred to as "a son of the Revolution" and "a child of Destiny."

Napoleon was so short that he would have had trouble seeing parades if he hadn't always been in them. One way he had of getting a better view was to sit on top of a horse on top of a hill. He kept his hair combed over part of his forehead so that people couldn't tell from the furrows in his brow whether he

Child of destiny

was worried. His favorite posture was with one hand inside his vest. Apparently he wanted to be ready for a sudden itch. You wouldn't call him handsome, unless you were one of his lieutenants and bucking for a captaincy.

Napoleon's uniforms were dashing, and he had a hard time keeping up with them. His trousers were dangerously tight, while his jacket sometimes caused him to be confused with the head usher. He wore epithets on his shoulders and a big bullet-proof medal over his heart. From the beginning, he put his hat on sideways, and no one ever dared tell him.

In spite of his appearance, Napoleon rose rapidly in rank. He became a general while people were still calling him "the little corporal." [1]

MARRIAGE TO JOSEPHINE

Napoleon's first marriage was to Josephine, who was six years older than Napoleon, as he began to notice as time went on.

Josephine was a widow, but blameless. Her first husband had been a bit of a rake, always promising to turn over a new leaf. A Creole by birth, her special brand of Southern hospitality had a way of bringing out the beast in men.

A few days after their marriage, Napoleon went on a campaign in Italy. Not many men get away so fast. He wrote a letter a day to Josephine, mostly nagging her to have a son.

[1] What they may have meant was that he was "a little corpulent."

She pointed out the difficulties, with him always away, but he was insistent. "Why do I have to do *everything*?" he asked in a tender passage in one of his letters.

Finally Napoleon grew tired of this unproductive correspondence and divorced Josephine. He then married an Austrian woman who gave him a son instead of an argument.

Napoleon deep in thought

NAPOLEON S CAMPAIGNS

1. *Italian Campaign.* It was clever of Napoleon to fight the Austrians in Italy where they did not understand the language and grew homesick for apple strudel. Dragging his cannon behind him, he marched straight over the Alps, enjoying some beautiful scenery and gaining momentum as he slid down into Italy. This filled his cannon with snow, but the Element of Surprise was so great that, fortunately, he did not have to fire it.

2. *Egyptian Campaign.* After subduing the Austrians in Italy, Napoleon encountered the Turks in Egypt, although he had gone there to fight the English. He got so he wasn't surprised at anything. The most interesting part of the Egyptian Campaign was the Battle of the Pyramids, in which Napoleon's army crouched behind one pyramid and the Turks behind an-

other. How Napoleon finally won is known as the Riddle of the Sphinx.

3. *English Campaign.* Napoleon roused the ire of the English by calling them "a nation of shoplifters." He then collected boats in a harbor across the Channel and seemed about to attack. Actually he had no intention of attacking, but was only collecting boats, the way some people collect stamps and matchbooks.

4. *Russian Campaign.* The farther Napoleon got into Russia, the more homesick he got for France. He was a pretty finicky conqueror by this time, and didn't like either the roads or the climate around Moscow. So he headed back toward Paris, and

Napoleon outside Moscow

could hardly wait to get onto cobblestones again. However, it was winter, and many of his men had left their long woollies in Montparnasse. Napoleon rode back through the snow at the head of his troops, as he always did when retreating, and kept one hand in his coat, this time to protect it from frostbite. The Russians continually attacked his rear, which was exposed, and cut his army into ribbons (campaign ribbons).

5. *Campaign at Sea.* Napoleon was better on land than in the water. His navy was repeatedly sunk by Lord Nelson, a full admiral who is not to be confused with his brother, Half

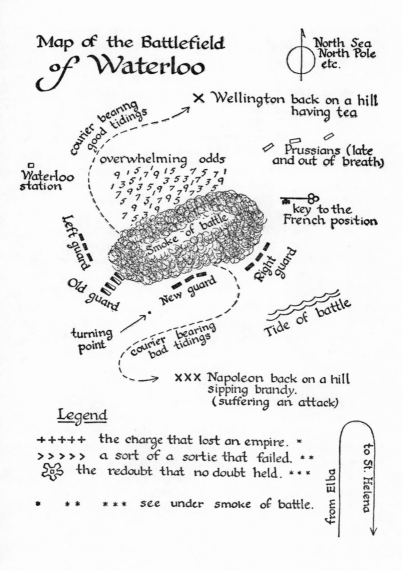

Map of the Battlefield of Waterloo

North Sea
North Pole
etc.

courier bearing good tidings

✕ Wellington back on a hill having tea

overwhelming odds

Prussians (late and out of breath)

Waterloo station

9 15 7 9 15 7 5 7 1
1 3 5 7 9 3 5 3 7 3 9
7 9 3 5 9 3 7 7 3 5 9
5 7 9 3 1 7 9 5
7 5 3 9

key to the French position

Smoke of battle

Left guard

Old guard

New guard

Right guard

turning point

courier bearing bad tidings

Tide of battle

✕✕✕ Napoleon back on a hill sipping brandy.
(suffering an attack)

Legend

+ + + + + the charge that lost an empire. *
> > > > > a sort of a sortie that failed. * *
✿ the redoubt that no doubt held. * * *

*   * *   * * * see under smoke of battle.

from Elba

to St. Helena

Nelson. This British seadog had only one eye, which he kept fixed on Lady Hamilton. Sometimes he looked through a telescope with his blind eye, which revealed great courage but not much else. Nelson was finally killed by a taxi while crossing Trafalgar Square, and a monument was erected on the spot.

NAPOLEON MEETS HIS WATERLOO

The Tide finally turned against Napoleon, and after his defeat at Leipzig it washed him up on the Island of Elba. But even in defeat he was clever. He said, "Able was I ere I saw Elba," which is "Elba saw I ere I was able" written backward. This is something you can't do with "They shall not pass."

Shortly thereafter, Napoleon left Elba, promising to be back in exactly One Hundred Days. Gathering up soldiers as he went along, he hurried to Waterloo, where Wellington was nervously looking at his watch and waiting for the Rendezvous with Destiny to begin.

On the way to the battlefield, Napoleon hurled back a Prussian core that had been thrown at him, and things looked promising. But Wellington came swooping down from Waterloo Station with a huge army of Englishmen with bristling mustaches, known as Overwhelming Odds. He was joined by Blücher, who arrived a little late because of trouble he was having with a new pair of shoes, and together they achieved a Resounding Victory. Napoleon retired to the island of Saint Helena, where he spent his remaining days preparing his *Memoirs*, in which he figured prominently. He was often seen strolling along the beach with his head bowed, muttering "Old emperors never die, they just fade away."

Ultimately Napoleon became sickening and was given a permanent room in the Hôtel des Invalides. Tourists say of it that it's a nice place to visit but they wouldn't want to live there.

THIRD TEST

1. Which was the smallest Louis? Is he the one who was called Shrimp Louis?

2. What did Madame de Maintenon, Madame de Pompadour, and Madame du Barry have in common? Which one had the most?

3. Wasn't Ivan terrible?

4. Analyze Peter the Great. Psychoanalyze Catherine the Great.

5. Discuss at length, and with specific gravity, the theory of falling bodies. What is the relationship between falling bodies and rolling heads?

6. Did Frederick the Great have any other pipe dreams besides his wish to become a famous flute player?

7. Arrange in some other order:

    (*a*) Jean

    (*b*) Jacques

    (*c*) Rousseau

8. Consider the advantages and disadvantages of being either, both, or neither of the following:

    (*a*) A noble savage

    (*b*) A savage noble

9. If Lord Nelson had only one arm, how did he keep the upper hand?

10. Has it ever occurred to you that Napoleon is the only general who ever met his Waterloo at Waterloo?

CHAPTER XXVIII

EUROPE AFTER NAPOLEON

AS SOON AS Napoleon was disposed of, a meeting was held in Vienna to divide the spoils before they became a menace to health. Europe was in a ferment.

At the Congress of Vienna, as the meeting was called, delegates waltzed and promenaded up and down staircases until they turned the affair into a Glittering Spectacle. Most statesmen were accompanied by beautiful women who stuffed handkerchiefs and secret papers into their bosoms.

The Congress of Vienna

One of the leaders at the Congress of Vienna was Tallyho, a foxy Frenchman. Another was Metternich, the Blue Bird, a master of intrigue who was studying for his doctorate. Tallyho and Metternich were always playing tricks—card tricks, rope tricks, and especially dirty tricks.

RETURN OF THE BOURBONS

The Bourbon kings got back on the throne of France, but a bit unsteadily.[1] There was one more Louis, the Eighteenth, and

[1] The Bourbons never did anything by halves, only by fifths.

another Charles, the Thirty-seventh at least. This Charles was stiff-necked and could look in only one direction, backward. He was finally driven from the throne and went to England, where, since they already had a king, he was surplus.

RETURN OF THE NAPOLEONS

Louis Napoleon was blessed with a combination of names that was irresistible to the French. To further his hold on the people, he named his first daughter Eclair. This nephew of Napoleon the Great was the pretender to the throne. After a while he stopped pretending and took over.

Louis Napoleon, or Napoleon III to those who may be keeping track, is best known for beautifying Paris and for marrying Eugénie with the light brown hair. Napoleon was something of a dandy, with a mustache which he waxed at both ends. Otherwise it would have been pointless. As for Eugénie, this gay

Napoleon III

creature kept the palace full of bright lights and laughter, both of them at Napoleon's expense.

The downfall of Napoleon III came in the Franco-Prussian War (see below). As befitted a man who came to power by a coup, he was captured in a Sedan.

———◆———

CHAPTER XXIX

INDUSTRIAL REVOLUTION

WE NOW COME to the Era of the Machine, when revolutions took place in factories instead of palaces. Whereas formerly there had been revolutions every few years, there were now revolutions per minute.

The Industrial Revolution

Industry was taken out of the home. People worked hard at the factory, in shifts, and then came home and flopped down on the sofa, shiftless. This was known as lazy-fare. The man of the house took off his shirt and shoes, and for hours did nothing but read the newspaper, if he could read, or snap his suspenders, if he couldn't. Fortunes were made by industrialists, especially those who manufactured suspenders.

ECONOMISTS AND OTHERS

About this time a number of economists arose. One of the first on his feet was Adam Smith. His book, *A Wealth of Notions*, is full of interesting ideas. One of these is that labor is more important than money; in other words, the main thing is to keep busy, even if you don't get paid. He believed in mass production, and was dead set against birth control.

Another important thinker was Thomas Malthus. Population, he thought, was outrunning the food supply, and something needed to be done about it. He suggested plowing people under instead of crops, and strongly advocated war and disease. Malthus was never elected to public office.

Finally there was Charles Darwin, the Original of the Species. Working on his theory of evolution, Darwin started with plants, although he believed that almost everyone else started with animals. He traced the evolution of man through the lower animals, such as the dachshund, and on up to the higher ones, like the giraffe. Darwin believed in heredity and was always pointing out how people inherited things like brown eyes, flat feet, and money.

Charles Darwin and a lower animal

THE IRON INDUSTRY

Iron began to come into its own, where it should have been all the time. Smelt iron was increasingly in evidence, particularly when the wind was blowing in your direction. Pig iron was widely used in the making of piggy banks. Cast iron was thrown from one worker to another and caught in buckets. Occasionally the workers would gang up and throw it at the mill owner.

After a while people became dissatisfied with iron and made steel out of it. Steel was harder than iron, as you could tell by biting first a bar of one and then a bar of the other. It was even predicted that in another few years the steel bar would replace the chocolate bar.

This was, in many ways, the Age of Steam. Steam was invented by James Watt and further developed by his son, Kilo. With the help of McAdam, they paved the way for better transportation. Soon the steam engine replaced the stagecoach, and the steam whistle replaced the whinny.

An early steam engine

Steam in time was superseded by electricity, which was invented by three dwarfs named Amp, Ohm, and Erg, the last a particularly repulsive little fellow. Nevertheless steam continued to have its uses, being better than electricity for pressing pants, opening envelopes, and inhaling when your nose is stopped up.

The textile industry was revolutionized by Spinning Jenny, a woman who went around like mad and could spin eight threads at a time. She kept this up for years, and every night slept like a top. Others who tried to keep pace with Jenny suffered dizzy spells. Fortunately a power loom was invented which employed the principle of the warp and kept the woof from the door.

We should not fail to mention a bright inventor by the name of Richard Arklight. It was he who, in a moment of horseplay, accidentally discovered how to make horsepower without horses.

A WAVE OF REFORM

People began to notice what was termed "man's inhumanity to man" and to think something similar should be done for women. Many took to reading the great German philosophers, Schope and Hauer, and became more depressed than ever. The next thing people knew they were engulfed by a Wave of Reform.

The climax of the Reform Wave came when the Corn Laws were repealed and it was no longer illegal to pick up the cob in your fingers.[1] Farmers, however, continued to keep an ear to the ground.

CHAPTER XXX

ITALY BECOMES ITALY

THE WAY THE map had been redrawn at the Congress of Vienna made Italy a collection of small and irregular pieces, good only for jigsaw puzzles. Oppressed by Austria, Italians were forced into such indignities as singing operas in German. Ardent patriots thought that if Italy could be made all one country, and run exclusively by Italians, there would be more uniformity in the proportion of spaghetti to meat balls.

Some Italians wanted war; others wanted pizza. The Italians had a small army, wearing uniforms left over from a musical comedy, and the only way they could make the Austrians keep their distance was by eating garlic. Had gas masks been available, the Austrians would have taken over the country lock, stock, and wine barrel.

The Italian statesmen and ministers, called *minestrone*, were in the soup and could see no way out. A few million Italians

[1] Appropriately enough, the fight was led by Richard Cobden.

managed to get to America on Quotas. Others got there on ships, taking with them their most precious possessions, such as hand organs, monkeys, and pushcarts loaded with oranges and bananas.

ITALIAN PATRIOTS

Fortunately for the future of Italy, several great leaders arose in their hour of need. We do not know the exact hour, or what they needed, but they apparently had synchronized their watches. These men, all of them full of patriotic ardor and *chianti*, included Mazzini, Cavour, and O. Sole Mio. Mazzini, a man of personal magnetism, picked up followers wherever he went. Cavour remained steadfast, despite enemies at home and some unpleasant foreign relations.

Three Italian patriots

The most colorful character in the struggle for unification was Gary Baldy, an Italian general who suffered from a receding hairline. He also had an olive complexion, as a result of chewing his Martinis. This dashing military leader was always dashing somewhere, usually with a large army right behind him. Sometimes it was his own. He won freedom and unity for Italy at last, but the Victor was Emmanuel II.

CHAPTER XXXI

BISMARCK

OTTO VON BISMARCK was a Prussian, and militaristic to the corps. During his student days he was quick to challenge to a duel, and always at swords' points with his fellows. From constantly lifting heavy sabers and beer steins he developed a rugged physique which enabled him to perform incredible feats of endurance, such as listening to the music of Wagner for hours on end.

As soon as he could, Bismarck grew a large mustache which effectively hid the saber scars and Mercurochrome stains on his face, neck, and chest. It also hid his emotions. Pictures of Bismarck invariably show him in uniform, since there are no pictures of him taking a bath. His tunic had a high collar, which afforded extra room for medals.

Bismarck

Early in his career Bismarck was summoned to court. The king was lonesome and wanted someone with whom he could sing *Ist das nicht ein Schnitzelbank?* When he heard young Bismarck's deep voice come in with *Ja, das ist ein Schnitzelbank,* he offered him a lifetime supply of herrings to stay on as court baritone. Thenceforth Bismarck stuck with the king through thick and thin, for bitters or for wurst. The king promoted Bismarck through the ranks from Pfc. to Prince, and in return Bismarck made the king an emperor.

Bismarck dearly loved war. He kept his soldiers practicing the goose step until the geese themselves were put to shame and flew south. The time he defeated the Austrians in the Seven Weeks' War he stepped up the cadence. One reason for Bismarck's fondness for war may have been that he was a Junker, and wanted to increase the supply of scrap.

Bismarck's greatest military triumph was the Franco-Prussian War. The French were soundly defeated, and the Germans occupied Paris. Since Paris was also occupied by the French, the housing shortage was acute.

In his old age Bismarck suffered from hardening of the arteries and came to be known as the Iron Chancellor. Finally he retired from government and became the capital of North Dakota.

———◆———

CHAPTER XXXII

RUSSIA UNDER THE CZARS

LIFE IN RUSSIA continued to be more backward than in other parts of Europe, possibly because of military reverses. Serfs were still chained to the soil, and cannot be blamed for singing depressing songs and accompanying themselves on their *ukases* and other odd-shaped instruments.

The Czars at this time were all either Romanoffs or Onandoffs. They lived in great splendor, usually up to their elbows in caviar. The most difficult of their daily tasks was removing all the medals before sending a uniform to the cleaner.

Because of their night-club pallor, the Czars were called White Russians. They had another reason to be pale, with so many annihilists lurking in the vicinity. The bombs then in use were round with a fuse sticking out, and handy for throwing at Czars. Czars who seemed to be bowing to the crowds as they rode by in their carriages were really ducking.

One Czar who died a natural death was Alexander III, but he saw no particular advantage in it. He was followed by Nicholas II, the last of the Czars, who reverted to the old custom.

A Czar ducking

CRIMEAN WAR

Russia tried to take some of the Black Sea away from Turkey. This looked easy, because the Turks were called The Sick Men of Europe. However the British, who were in excellent health, came to the aid of the Turks and proved to the Russians that Crimea doesn't pay.

It was during the Crimean War that Florence Nightingale, the inventor of nurses, made a name for herself by singing to soldiers in hospitals. She went from one poor wretch to another, helping them suffer. On one of her nightly rounds she stubbed her toe on a bedpan and thereafter was known as "the lady with the limp."

This was also the war in which Alfred Lord Tennyson led the Light Brigade into the Valley of Death, from which he

"Someone had blundered"

alone escaped alive. He might also have escaped criticism, but he blundered and wrote a poem about it that many have been forced to memorize.

RUSSO-JAPANESE WAR

Russia was looking for a small-sized war and Japan seemed to serve the purpose. But the Japanese, with Oriental cunning and a large navy, struck first. In a short time the Russians had suffered defeat on both land and sea, and a peace was arranged to put an end to their suffering. The Russians, who were still pretty crude, went home licking their wounds.

A curious thing about the Russo-Japanese War is that it began in China and ended in Portsmouth, New Hampshire. The reason for the latter was that the United States offered its good offices, which had indirect lighting and air conditioning.

RASPUTIN

We could not conclude this chapter without mention of Rasputin, a mad monk with an hypnotic eye. It didn't seem to trouble him, but it played hell with those he looked at. Rasputin also had an eye, possibly the same one, for the ladies. There was something about his tousled hair, untrimmed beard, and the buttons missing from his coat that made them want to mother him.

Political complications arose when the Czarina came under Rasputin's spell. He gave orders to the Czarina, the Czarina gave orders to the Czar, the Czar to the generals, and so on down to the common soldier, who muttered to himself. There was some suspicion that Rasputin wasn't really a monk at all, because he never took orders.

Rasputin and friend

A group of nobles finally did away with Rasputin by giving him poison and then stabbing him to make sure. A few skeptics stood around with clubs.

———◆———

CHAPTER XXXIII

CIVILIZATION ON THE MARCH

THIS BRINGS US to the Modern Era, characterized by the way everything was on the march. Science was on the march. Empires were on the march. Armies were on the march. Fortunes were made in the manufacture of corn pads, and there was a callous disregard for human life. One of those on the march

Gladstone and his bag

was Gladstone, the British Prime Minister, who sometimes took along his wife, a large woman with a rather rough exterior who was known as Gladstone's Bag.

In the scientific field the most significant advances were made by the French. Usually it was men who made advances but occasionally women. They worked all night in their laboratories. One great scientist was Pasture, who found a way of getting milk out of bottles instead of cows. He also tested test tubes and now and then bit a dog to see if it made him mad.

Almost as important was the work of Madame Curie, who invented radium and made it possible to tell time in the dark, provided you had a watch with you. At the time of her death she was painting a luminous substance on sundials to improve their effectiveness at night.

COLONIALIZATION

Because of science, people began to live longer and look younger and take up more room than if they had died and lain still. Countries like England, France, Italy, and Germany began to send their surplus people to places like Africa, many of them disguised as missionaries. They went fearlessly forward into backward countries and came out with ivory and butterflies and people like Dr. Livingstone I. Presume.

The British, spearheaded by Rudyard Kipling, soon had a far-flung empire, on which the sun, for some obscure reason, never set. The British were especially aided by Gunga Gin, a better man than most, who kept everyone supplied with gin and quinine water. He eased the pain of the dying and helped them take their shots.

Gunga Gin and Sahib

The white man's burden, consisting largely of tea and crumpets and pictures of Queen Victoria, was increasingly borne by native bearers.

CHAPTER XXXIV

THE KAISER

WILLIAM II, sometimes called Vilhelm, was best known as the Kaiser. He could be recognized by his mustache, which turned up unexpectedly, just as the Kaiser often did. Another distinguishing feature was the iron spike on top of his hat. This made him look like a unicorn when he lowered his head.

Unfortunately for the rest of the world, the Kaiser had built up a large army and navy that needed some practical experience. Warehouses were full of wound stripes which had

The Kaiser

not been issued. Unless he could find an excuse for a war pretty soon, the Kaiser feared his standing army might slump into a sitting position. The excuse came when a Serb, hiding behind a powder keg in the Balkans, shot the arch Duke of Austria in his carriage. The Kaiser blew up, shouting such German expletives as *Donder!* and *Blitzen!* He could be heard across the Channel, where the English, living in Splendid Isolation, had not heard such shocking language since before the Victorian Era.

WORLD WAR I

Countries began to choose up sides, selecting the big, strong countries first and gradually coming down to the little fellows who wore glasses. Some of the smallest and weakest countries thought they would never get chosen and had their feelings hurt.

World War I was the first war to be numbered. It is not known why this convenient device was not employed earlier. If it had, this might have been World War CXLVIII. The conflict began when Austria-Hungary declared war on Serbia,[1] which tried to confuse the issue by declaring war on Germany. However, Germany cleverly retaliated by declaring war on Russia and, just to make sure, on France as well. From then on there was a declaration of war every few days, including declarations by some countries which preferred declaring to warring. For a while the Allies had more countries on their side than soldiers.

REVERSES AND VICTORY

Things went against the Allies at first, and the Germans almost took Paris. But the Allies gathered up a vast army of old French taxicab drivers, made fearless by years of coping with the traffic around the Place de la Concorde. They advanced on the Germans bumper to bumper, sounding their horns continuously, and the enemy fled in terror. It was a great victory but costly, since the French kept their meters ticking.

[1] Which has since disappeared, and there is no use looking for it.

A fierce French taxi driver

The remainder of the war was fought in trenches, where the outnumbered Allies kept their chins up and their heads down and waited for the Americans. This was to become an Old European Custom.

There were two fronts, the Eastern Front and the Western Front, and presumably the same number of rears. For a time it was all quiet on the Western Front and writers were able to get a head start on such postwar novels as *A Farewell to Armentières*.[1] At sea, the Germans tried to close the sea lanes and starve the British, not realizing that the British had had years of experience eating food that no one else would touch.

Finally, with the coming of fresh American troops,[2] the Germans began to see the Folly of War. Young boys dreamed of home and could be heard to mutter, *"Mutter."* Even cruel, merciless generals like Von Wienerschnitzel and Von Sauerbraten wanted to get back to the Fatherland to see whether they had become fathers.

At last the Germans quit. Some laid down their arms, others raised their hands. The Kaiser, whom the Americans had been hanging in Effigy as well as in Scranton and Peoria, escaped

---

[1] Written by the author of that tender novel of domestic life, *My Son Also Rises*.

[2] So considered by the young women of France.

A retired despot

to Holland with his neck. He also took along several members
of his family, an ax, and a pile of cordwood. He lived for many
years in Holland, chopping his wood into smaller and smaller
pieces and having his picture taken each year on his birthday.
Eventually he came to be known as a kindly old man, proving
that time heals all wounds provided they are not fatal to start
with.

———◆———

CHAPTER XXXV

THE RUSSIAN REVOLUTION

SHORTLY BEFORE the end of World War I the Czar of Russia
was removed. Everyone breathed easier except the Czar, who
stopped breathing entirely.

This was the signal for the Revolution. It was led by two
different age groups, the Boysheviks and the Mensheviks, both
of them having spent the war years collecting bombs and growing beards. As soon as they had sufficient bombs and their
beards were long enough to hide their sinister intentions, they
struck.

105

A bomb collector

MARX AND LENIN

The ideas behind the Revolution came from Karl Marx. Because of his German dialect and his love of possessions, he made speeches that were full of Dialectical Materialism. Marx advocated making the poor rich and the rich poor; that is, leveling classes and flattening anybody who objected.

One of the most enthusiastic followers of Marx was Lenin. Although he was a Russian and Marx was a German, they felt that they were brothers under the skin. (Since they were both thick-skinned, the feeling ran deep.) Lenin was anti-capitalist but pro-letariate. A labor leader and a proponent of the closed shop, his greatest achievement was founding the Soviet Union and closing the shops of thousands of businessmen. Once in power, he made the Communist Party the only legal party in order to avoid confusion at the polls. Another thing that helped was having only one candidate. Lenin inflamed his followers [1] with such slogans as "Workers of the world, ignite." He sang a song of his own composition, *The Irrationale*, until the day of his death, which many thought untimely in that it should have come sooner.

TROTSKY

After Lenin's death there was a tug-of-war for power. Two of those who had the most pull were Stalin (see below) and Trotsky. Trotsky, a little man who went around at a jog,

---

[1] Causing them to be known as Reds.

Trotsky

something between a walksky and a runsky, replaced the old-fashioned Samovars with Commissars.

He had trouble, however, with his Party Line, not knowing that Stalin was listening in. Stalin was always purging his friends, giving them a bottle of his special home remedy and saying, "Take this and it will fix you up." Trotsky outwitted Stalin, however, by dying violently in Mexico instead of Moscow.

———◆———

CHAPTER XXXVI

MUSSOLINI
ill

BENITO MUSSOLINI, called the Ill Duce by those who thought he looked slightly sallow and swollen, was the Original Fascist. He became popular in Italy by urging everyone to wear a black shirt, which led to a substantial reduction in laundry bills.

Before he became Dictator, Mussolini was a Socialist Firebrand. He frequently made the headlines, especially during the period when he was a newspaper editor. During World War 1 he rose to the rank of corporal and began to detect a certain similarity between himself and Napoleon.

Mussolini is remembered for his gleaming boots and head. It is said that he used the same polish on both. He is also remembered for his jutting jaw. He loved to stand on a balcony, with his hand in the air, and jut it. Crowds gathered to watch.

Ill Duce

MUSSOLINI'S WARS

Mussolini believed in living dangerously. Since this could best be done during a war, and since the Ethiopians had only spears and shields with which to defend themselves,[1] he unhesitatingly engaged the Ethiopians in battle. The sharp-tongued Ethiopian emperor, Highly Sassy, took refuge under his umbrella and tried to confuse Mussolini by changing the name of his country to Abyssinia. But owing to the courage of the Italian airmen, who dropped their bombs on the natives despite the risk of being hit by rocks, Mussolini won his first war and his second chest-full of medals.

Mussolini used his next war, which was between the Loyalists

[1] He didn't believe in living *too* dangerously.

and the Disloyalists in Spain, to get the bugs out of some of his new equipment, such as tanks, guns, and sleeping bags.

Having won two and lost none, Mussolini was leading the league. He also had the trains running on time and was able to be on the platform with a band whenever Hitler (see below) arrived. He tried hard to be Hitler's friend, and was unhappy when Adolf insisted on bringing a bodyguard.

The last war for Mussolini was World War II, and it was one too many. Hitler suggested that he fight some of the smaller countries first, such as Greece, but forgot to tell him that the Greeks, unlike the Ethiopians, had guns. Soon after the Americans got in, Mussolini got out.

———◆———

CHAPTER XXXVII

HITLER

HEIL HITLER, the German Furor, was born a Schicklgruber but outgrew it. Other unfortunate tendencies, however, such as starting wars and failing to shave his upper lip, he never got over.

In one of his early pictures, when he was a corporal[1] in World War I, he stood at the extreme left. There he was so frightened by a Communist that he moved over to the extreme right. Wherever he was he was a Fanatic, or extremely extreme.

Hitler's great ambition was to become an artist, and he dreamed of a life of easel. However he was forced by circumstances, chief among which were the art critics, to become a house painter.

HITLER'S EARLY CAREER

With a Munich friend of his named Putsch, he gathered up an army of young men called Storm Troopers who liked to

[1] See Napoleon and Mussolini, above. This is getting monotonous.

The disappointed artist

splash around in the rain. Hitler toughened them for the hard days ahead by forcing them to listen to his speeches. He also made them hold their right hand up and look to one side while marching. Hitler was leading them to war, but this way they could not tell where they were going.

One of Hitler's attempts to seize the government was abortive. He was caught and thrown into prison, where he suffered keenly from confinement and wrote his autobiography, *Mein Kramps*. At first the book sold slowly, but after Hitler became Dictator it was the German Book-of-the-Month Club choice every month for three years. Those who owned fewer than thirty-six copies were suspected of having no feeling for literature. Such unfortunate persons were ineligible for the Book Club bonus, an autographed photo of the Furor.

HITLER BECOMES DICTATOR

The President of Germany at this time was von Hindenburg, named after a famous dirigible and sometimes referred to as Colonel Blimp. He had been threatening to dissolve the Reichstag, but this was at best a slow process. Hitler burned the place down overnight and became such a national hero that von Hindenburg offered to make him Dictator. Hitler accepted, and von Hindenburg spent his remaining years experimenting with new shapes for pretzels.

Hitler promptly instituted Sweeping Reforms. He built himself a balcony like Mussolini's (though he fell a bit short in developing a bay window), composed a song in honor of an overworked baritone named Hoarse Vessel, and invented the Big Lie.[1] He also frequently entertained his friends with imitations of Charlie Chaplin.

Adolf as Charlie

HITLER STARTS A WAR

All this time Hitler had been living in an eagle's nest at Berchtesgaden. Finally he got tired of fighting off the mother eagle every night. Anyway he decided Germany needed more space for housing developments and roads on which he could drive his folks' wagon.

Hitler's technique was to divide and conquer. This was a change from the traditional method of conquer and divide. With the help of General von Blitzkrieg, a corps of Panthers,

[1] He failed to patent it, however, and it has been used by dictators and demagogues ever since.

a Desert Fox, and the Luft Waffle, he felt he could not lose. After consulting his horrorscope and picking up some gruesome ideas, he was off.

———————◆———————

CHAPTER XXXVIII

WORLD WAR II

WORLD WAR II was also called the the Total War, the Global War, and the War to End Wars to End Wars. For a while it was called the Phoney War and was fought at long distance. The busiest men at the front were the foreign correspondents. Even though they filed their dispatches, most accounts were longer than necessary.

Many hoped the war might be ended before it began, which would have shortened it considerably. The British leader, Sir Never Chainberlin, believed he had secured peace in our time, but our time was not the same as his time because in England it was later than he thought. He believed he had carried the day, when actually he had carried only his umbrella.

THE WAR AT ITS HEIGHT

The war was soon raging, as was Hitler. When things went bad for him he chewed rugs to disguise his nervousness. During prolonged retreats there was nothing left on the floor of his office but a few slightly bent carpet tacks.

The French stayed behind the Imaginary Line, where they were perfectly safe until the enemy decided to cross it. The most serious problem for the French was caused by the collaborators, men who volunteered to ghost-write Hitler's memoirs.

The English, meanwhile, were going through their Finest Hour, which lasted several months. While bombs rained down on them, Londoners remained calm and collected their insurance. Prime Minister Churchill, remembering that the Ger-

Winny and companions

mans relied on blood and iron, urged his countrymen to go the enemy one better with blood, sweat, and tears. Only one grave question remains about this great British leader: did he make more history than he wrote, or vice versa?

In North Africa, the British had their backs to the wall and were running low on tea. To keep up morale, Field Marshal Montgunnery, their commander, carried a swagger stick, although in a crisis he could swagger without one. Demands began to be heard for a Second Front, the first one being too close for comfort. Churchill suggested an attack on the Soft Underbelly of Europe, to be called Operation Abdominal.

It was a Grave Moment in history.

FINAL PHASE

Things began to go against the Axes when the Nastis invaded Russia. This was meant to be a surprise, but Hitler had shown his hand by signing a Friendship Pact. The Russians employed the scorched-earth policy. Whereas Napoleon had found Russia too cold, Hitler found it too hot. He headed back for Germany, leaving the Russians smoldering with resentment and almost out of matches.

The war came to a swift conclusion when the Americans got into it (see World War I, above). As soon as they had established beachheads and PX's, and could assure the troops an adequate supply of comic books, they advanced rapidly up Italy and across France. Eventually they met the Russians at the Elbe, where they shook hands, exchanged cigarettes,[1] and had their pictures taken. This became known as the High Point in American-Russian relations.

As for Hitler, when last heard of he was trapped in a bunker in Berlin, looking for his number ten iron. Some believe he is still alive, having escaped by breast stroke to South America where he is speculating in beef and suppressing newspapers.

Having come to one end in Europe, the war came to another end in Asia when Emperor Hirohito became disheartened on being told he was not divine. Whatever else is said about World War II, it is the only war with two ends.

———◆———

CHAPTER XXXIX

STALIN

JOSEPH STALIN, or Uncle Joe, was born in Georgia. He left there at an early age, however, and spoke Russian without a trace of a Southern accent. His original name was Joseph Vissarionovich Dzhugashvili, which he did away with because it was too long to get on the ballot. Later, just to play safe, he did away with the ballot.

As a boy, Stalin was expelled from school for always tinkering with bombs (he worked his way up from water to stink to incendiary) instead of doing his homework. Before expelling the lad, they suspended him, but the rope broke. His teachers said nothing good would ever come of him, and his classmates voted him the Student Most Likely to Blow Himself Up.

Once out of school, Stalin became known for his revolutionary exploits. He always worked hand in glove with Lenin in order not to leave fingerprints.

[1] This was the first of a series of incidents in which the Russians got the better of it.

*Working hand
in glove*

STALIN GAINS CONTROL

Eventually Stalin inherited Lenin's mantle. However, it was a bit large for him, and he preferred to wear the simple uniform of a Generalissimissimo. To make sure he would not forget his instructions, he wore the orders of Lenin on his left breast.

To speed production, Stalin gave awards to workers who kept their minds on their work and produced large families. Each medal bore the inscription, "First in Fertility." Someone thought of naming these and other awards Joseph Stalin Prizes, and was awarded a Joseph Stalin Prize for the originality of his idea. He was also given a picture of Stalin to put on his living-room wall if he could find a spot where he did not already have one.

A believer in system, Stalin instituted a series of Five-Year Plans whereby a certain number of his rivals would be done away with during each period. Officials who wanted to stay out of trouble busied themselves with the task of changing the names of cities and streets to Stalingrad, Stalino, Stalinabad, and Stalinagood.

STALIN MAKES RUSSIA A WORLD POWER

Stalin had an insatiable lust for power which drove him to build enormous dams and hydroelectric projects. Among the many groups Stalin liquidated were the Klucks (rich farmers), the Young Republicans of Moscow, and Minsky's Burleski.

A collectivist, Stalin soon acquired all the neighboring countries, beginning with small ones like Lithuania, Latvia, and Upper Slobovia. Russia became so big that there was room on the map to call it Union of Soviet Socialist Republics in large letters.

STALIN'S DEATH

The Communists began to believe that Stalin was immortal. But something went wrong and he died. Post offices throughout Russia were alerted for another change in the names of streets and cities.

CHAPTER XL

THE COLD WAR

THERE WERE ACTUALLY two Cold Wars, one against the Common Cold and the other between the East and the West. Since the North and South had already fought it out, this was all that was left. Neither war has yet come to a conclusion, though experiments continue with antihistamines and explosives.

Many hoped the Cold War would be ended by the death of Stalin. But Malenkov actually went Stalin one better. He continued the double talk and the double cross and added the double chin. However, Malenkov himself was soon ousted, perhaps because he took up too much room in the reviewing stand.

At times the Cold War has become a War of Words.[1] At other times there is so much saber-rattling that the words are drowned out. But some credit must be given to the United Nations, which serves as a place for the meeting of minds, or

[1] The Communists, because they never keep their words, have plenty of them for others.

116

*Malenkov
took up
too much room*

at least of delegates. Despite some frightfully long speeches, the U.N. has proved that wars are better heard than fought.

CHAPTER XLI

CONCLUSION

WE HAVE NOW come from the beginning of Europe to as near the end of Europe as Europe was at the time this book was written. Looking ahead, we can only say that the future of man was never brighter, which is a terribly discouraging commentary on the past.

THE END

FOURTH AND FINAL TEST

1. Look back over all you have read. Do you see anything that looks better than Madame du Barry?

2. Which would be easier to pass, (*a*) a Reform Bill or (*b*) a Counterfeit Bill?

3. Sketch with a soft pencil the high points of Catherine the Great.

4. Estimate the approximate weight of the white man's burden.

5. Describe the difference between a black shirt, a brown shirt, and a hair shirt. Would the course of history have been changed if Hitler's troops had worn sweat shirts?

6. Suggest several destinations for a Fellow Traveler.

7. Is it true that history repeats itself? Does it also mumble?

8. Leave the following:
    (*a*) Margins
    (*b*) Test papers
    (*c*) The room quietly

SUGGESTED READING

The reader who has completed this book may, or quite understandably may not, wish to read further in the field of European history. Additional reading is strongly recommended, especially for anyone desiring to become a specialist, a bore, a history teacher, or all three.

In compiling a list of suggested reading, the author carefully combed the shelves of the local library. He was finally forced to give this up when several teeth came out of the comb and the librarian threatened to knock out a few more.

Unfortunately, the list of suggested reading was lost while the author was on safari in deepest, darkest Africa. If the list is recovered, it will be included in the next edition, along with a small piece of elephant tusk.

Meanwhile the serious student of history, and especially the overserious student, might profitably read this book again, from cover to cover, there being no cover charge. If he has learned to read between the lines, he will be able to go along at a great rate, with no words to slow him down.

ABOUT THE AUTHOR

Richard Armour is only one person, although he seems to be at least three. As Professor Armour (Ph.D., Litt.D.) he has taught in a number of colleges and universities, has lectured in Germany, has held research fellowships in England and France, and has written scholarly books of biography and literary criticism. As Colonel Armour he has served with troops and on the War Department General Staff and been several times decorated. As plain Richard Armour he is widely known as one of America's most popular writers of light verse and prose humor. He has contributed to more than seventy magazines, among them *The New Yorker* and *The Saturday Evening Post*. His books, of which this is the fourteenth, include the gay parody of American history *It All Started with Columbus*, a best seller now in its tenth printing, and the recently published *Light Armour*.

A Californian, Dr. Armour is now Professor of English at Scripps College and the Claremont Graduate School. He has, as he says, two costumes, "cap and gown and cap and bells."

817.5   Armour, Richard Willard
A   It all started with Europa; being an un-
        digested history of Europe from prehistoric
        man to the present, proving that we remember
        best whatever is least important.   Appropri-
        ately absurd illus. by Campbell Grant.
        McGraw, 1955.

            1. Europe - Hist. - Anec., fac., satire,
        etc.   I. T.